HOW TO HELP YOL ...OOL

In this Series

other titles in preparation

How To Books General Editor Roland Seymour

HELP YOUR CHILD AT SCHOOL

John West-Burnham

Northcote House

First published in 1987 by Northcote House Publishers Ltd, Harper & Row House, Estover Road, Plymouth PL6 7PZ, United Kingdom. Tel: Plymouth (0752) 705251. Telex: 45635. Fax: (0752) 777603.

British Library Cataloguing in Publication Data
West-Burnham, John
   How to help your child at school. — (How to books).
   1. Schools — England — Handbooks, manuals, etc.
   I. Title
   371'.00942 LA632

   ISBN 0-7463-0329-7

Printed and bound in Great Britain

Contents

Preface

This guide is intended to help develop that crucial relationship in the educational system — the partnership between parents and teachers. I believe that if this partnership is working effectively then almost all children will benefit from the skill and expertise of teachers and the resources available within schools. Without the involvement, interest and support of parents there is little that teachers can do.

I have therefore tried to provide information, advice and guidance to help parents understand an extremely complex and rapidly changing system. As you refer to this book you may be surprised at how much is involved in the life of a modern school of which you may have been unaware. Part of the object of this book is to cast light on this so that you can then play your part in partnership with the school. There can be no substitute for regular exchanges of information and the development of trust between parents and school which will be directly reflected in the attitudes of children.

Such a crucial relationship will inevitably break down at times and I have tried to indicate the procedures and tactics most likely to bring about the least damaging outcome and allow the best education possible for your son or daughter.

My thanks to Mrs Margaret Everall for her care in producing the manuscript; to my editor, Roland Seymour, for his interest and patience; and to Joss and Daniel for the inspiration.

John West-Burnham

1
The Education System of England

Education in England and Wales is free and compulsory for children between the ages of 5 and 16. Pupils may stay at school for a further 3 years after the age of 16.

The Department of Education and Science
The **Department of Education and Science** (DES) is more concerned with policy than administration. It has no direct responsibility for providing education services but does control:

- the national level of expenditure on education
- the amount of educational building
- the number and pay of teachers
- the development of new laws relevant to the education service

Her Majesty's Inspectorate (HMI) are responsible for monitoring the quality of education; they also provide the Secretary of State with specialist advice on the curriculum and on improving the quality of education.

There is a trend towards greater control of the education system by the DES. This is shown in much more specific control over how **Local Education Authorities** (LEAs) spend their money, clearer guidelines on what is to be taught and the setting up of **city colleges**.

Local Education Authorities
Education is provided by 105 Local Education Authorities; they own the school buildings, employ the teachers and provide the resources.

Local Education Authorities are run by **Education Committees** which are made up of councillors elected to county councils, outer London borough councils and the metropolitan district councils. The **Inner London Education Authority** (ILEA) is directly elected.

All LEAs appoint a **Chief Education Officer** and education officers who are responsible for the day-to-day administration of education. LEAs also appoint **advisers** who are responsible for the quality and development of teaching.

Education is paid for by a combination of rates and grants from central government, with most of it coming from the rates. However, this does not mean that LEAs are free to spend as they wish. Government approval is necessary for a wide range of expenditure.

Schools

The size, type and number of schools will be decided by each LEA subject to the approval of the Secretary of State. The names used to describe different types of schools and the ages they cater for vary significantly from one authority to another:

Pre-school education

Ages   3-4   Nursery

Compulsory education

Ages	5-7	Infant	or	Ages	5-9	Primary
	7-11	Primary			9-13	Middle
	11-16	Secondary			13-	Secondary

Post-compulsory education

Ages 16-19   Further   or   Tertiary

There are a number of other combinations possible but they will be variations on these themes. Another variation is selection at the age of 11. A few LEAs still maintain grammar schools and secondary modern schools.

Schools may be divided into two broad categories:

● those established and run by the LEAs
● those established by another body but financed by the LEA, usually known as **voluntary schools** and linked with the Church of England or Roman Catholic Church

Independent schools are privately owned and run, and set their own admission standards and fees to be charged. Some of these schools are in the **Assisted Places Scheme** under which the government pays a proportion of the fees.

Examination boards

Although subject to the overall approval of the DES the examination boards are independent bodies responsible for

- developing examination **syllabuses**
- setting and marking **examinations**
- awarding **certificates**

GCSE and A-level examinations are the responsibility of boards which are regionally based across England and Wales. Decisions about examination entry are taken by schools, subject to exam board regulations and LEA policy.

Post-school education

This sector covers a very wide range of institutions — tertiary colleges, colleges of further education, colleges of art, agricultural colleges, colleges of higher education, polytechnics and universities. There is an enormous variety of courses at differing levels with varying entry qualifications.

Age	Institution	Entry Qualifications	Award
16+	College of F. Education Tertiary College	Aptitude, college test	CPVE BTEC Certificate Craft Courses
16+	Tertiary College	4 x GCSE	A-levels BTEC Diploma
18+	Colleges of Higher Education Polytechnics	1-2 A-levels	Diplomas
	Universities	2-3 A-levels	Degrees

This table does not show the enormous variety of vocational courses available at 16+ validated by City & Guilds, and by the professional bodies.

2
Schools in Wales, Scotland and Northern Ireland

The education system of Wales, Scotland and Northern Ireland has many features in common with those of England, and there is a considerable degree of cross-referencing. However there are some significant differences.

Wales

For most purposes the Welsh educational system closely parallels the English, although it is the **Welsh Office** and not the DES which is the government department responsible.

Local Educational Authorities in Wales are exactly the same as those in England as far as powers, responsibilities and membership are concerned. Equally the qualifications and training of teachers are identical.

The curricula offered will be very similar, the only substantial difference being in the use of the **Welsh language**. In some schools it is the main medium of instruction in most subjects; in others it is optional. The balance of language in the curriculum should be a factor in choosing a school in Wales.

Scotland

The education system in Scotland is the responsibility of the **Secretary of State for Scotland,** administered through nine regional and three island authorities.

Although the Scottish system is broadly parallel to that of England and Wales there are significant differences of emphasis.

- **primary-secondary** transfer takes place at the age of twelve
- all Scottish secondary schools are **comprehensive**
- **religious education** is provided appropriate to the area in which a school is situated
- **Gaelic** is taught in some parts of the Highlands and Western Isles
- **examinations** at 16 and 18 are broadly the same as GCSE and A-levels

The Scottish educational system has a reputation for high academic and disciplinary standards. It has also pioneered many of the major changes in the curriculum later adopted in England and Wales.

Northern Ireland

Education in Northern Ireland is the responsibility of the **Secretary of State for Northern Ireland** and is administered through five Education and Library Boards which are broadly similar to LEAs in England and Wales.

There are a number of significant differences between education in Northern Ireland and the rest of Britain:

● there are **few comprehensives** — most areas operate a selection procedure for entry to grammar schools
● there are nearly twice as many **single-sex** schools
● there are two main types of schools — **voluntary** (largely controlled by the Roman Catholic Church) and **controlled** (which are run by the boards and largely Protestant in orientation)
● in both voluntary and controlled schools the clergy have the right to provide **denominational teaching,** otherwise the curriculum is very similar
● parents do **not** have the right to express a **preference** for a particular school

3
How Schools Work

It is easy to view schools as just a collection of teachers and classrooms. In fact they are usually extremely complex organisations. As with any large organisation it is important to know who has the responsibility and who has the power.

Schools are normally organised as hierarchies; this reflects the career structure of teachers and the need to delegate responsibility and specialisation.

A large **primary school** might be organised like this:

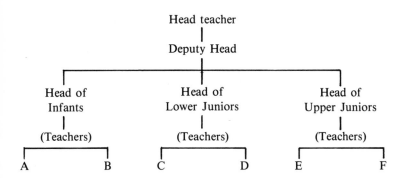

Within this structure teacher C might be responsible for music in the school, teacher E for maths and science and the head of upper juniors for language work.

Because of their size **secondary schools** are often much more complicated but the principles are the same. An example of the organisational structure of a secondary school is given on the next page.

There may well be a range of other roles, such as teachers in charge of resources, visits, or special needs. Almost all teachers will have at least two roles — as **subject** teachers and as part of the **pastoral** system.

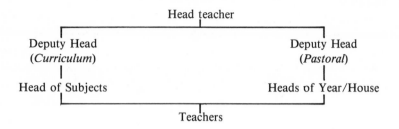

There are a number of key roles in primary and secondary schools.

Head teachers
In law head teachers have final responsibility for all aspects of school life and have significant powers to help them in this. They also have considerable discretion in how they run their schools. Some heads will spend a lot of their time teaching, others hardly any at all. Some will control every aspect of school life, others will delegate to other staff.

Deputy heads
Deputies usually have three broad functions — as classroom teachers, deputising for the headteacher, and having administrative and managerial functions in the school.

In primary schools deputies will spend most of their time teaching and carry out other functions in their 'spare' time.

Secondary deputies will spend a lot of their time administering and coordinating the work of other teachers. They will usually act with the full authority of the head and so be able to make decisions. However, the role and powers of deputies varies from school to school.

Heads of department
These are the 'middle' managers of schools. Usually they are responsible for a subject area in secondary schools and an age range in primary schools. They may also be known as Heads of Faculty in secondary schools. In all cases their responsibilities will include the development of their subject/age curriculum, coordination of teachers, control of resources and helping to develop school policies.

Heads of year/house
These are only found in secondary schools and are responsible for managing the pastoral system. This usually means oversight of pupils' progress, a general responsibility for their welfare, liaison with specialist agencies such as educational psychologists and almost all initial contact with parents.

Teachers

In primary schools teachers will be with their own class for most of the week, secondary teachers will teach an average of 80 per cent of the week, the rest of the time being used for marking and preparation and administrative duties. In both cases it is almost impossible to complete this work in school time.

Non-teaching staff

Schools are very dependent upon non-teaching staff for their effective working. Such staff will include technical assistants in laboratories and workshops, clerical and administrative staff, welfare assistants, canteen, caretaking and cleaning staff. All of these staff make a significant contribution to the well-being of children in school.

The **prospectus** issued by all schools will indicate how to contact teachers, and when. The **school secretary** is often the best source of information in the first instance. The crucial thing is to contact the right teachers at the right time.

Essential School Data

Do you have:

1 The address of the local education authority

2 The address of the district education office

3 The name of the head teacher

4 The address and telephone number of the school

5 The name of the chairman of Governors and parent-governors

6 The name of your child's class or form teacher and year/house head

7 Details of the school day

8 Information about travelling arrangements

9 Details of lunchtime arrangements

10 Arrangements for religious and sex education

Does the school have:
Relevant information about you and your circumstances?

4
How to Help Your Child at School

This section is divided into topics covering most aspects of school life and the queries raised and problems encountered most often by parents. Sometimes it it not possible to lay down clear guidelines as to how a child can be helped in a particular situation, or there might be a range of possibilities open to parents. So it can be useful to be aware of the background to a situation,

"Speak up, dad!"

or to know how a particular system has evolved. This section, then, sets out to give practical guidance wherever possible and also attempts to explain some of the complexities and anomalies of our education system. Parents who are well informed themselves are better able to help their children.

Accidents

Key points

- Responsibility for accidents
- Causes of accidents
- Safety requirements
- Preventative action

Schools are complex, busy places with a wide range of activities in progress. Some of these activities are potentially dangerous if supervision is inadequate or if children themselves fail to observe safety rules and guidelines. There are three main sets of circumstances where accidents are most likely to occur:

- travelling to and from school and around the school
- in the course of lessons
- on school trips

A teacher's responsibility extends to taking the same reasonable care of a child as a parent. However, the law recognises the differences between caring for one child and thirty-five, and the fact that children may not always obey instructions.

Travel

A headteacher has no responsibility for children travelling to and from school. It is now generally recognised that teachers become responsible for children on school premises *ten minutes before,* and remain responsible *ten minutes after,* the official school day.

Children who are sent to school very early, or by public transport, are thus *not* the responsibility of the school. Any accident is the responsibility of those actually involved and not the education system.

On school premises

Movement within the school is the responsibility of the staff and adequate supervision should be provided at appropriate times. However, no amount of supervision can prevent malicious activity or curb the exuberant hurly-burly of large numbers of children on the move. The crucial factor is the level of reasonable care displayed.

Lessons

There are a number of lessons where accidents are statistically more likely to occur — games and physical education, science, workshop lessons and domestic science.

Great care must be taken to distinguish between accidents resulting from a teacher's negligence, those resulting from children wilfully ignoring instructions, and genuine accidents.

All potentially dangerous activities should take place in the context of:

- qualified and competent teacher or instructor
- appropriate and properly maintained equipment
- clear guidelines and safety regulations
- children having appropriate clothing and equipment

If you are uncertain about the safety of a timetabled activity then seek reassurance from the school. Parents can also help by ensuring that their children meet guidelines for appropriate dress for games and observing rules about the wearing of jewellery, length of hair, etc. A teacher would be acting reasonably in refusing to allow a child to take part in an activity if he or she was not properly prepared or equipped. In cases of hardship schools may provide equipment or the LEA *may* be able to offer financial assistance.

Trips
Taking parties of children on an outing or away for a longer-term visit poses special problems. You will find a section on page 112 devoted to **Trips and visits.**

Take precautions
1. Ensure that the school has relevant **medical information** about your child, such as partial deafness, colour blindness, asthma, being subject to fits.

2. Provide **contact telephone numbers** for during the day plus an alternative number for a relative or neighbour if you are likely to be unavailable.

3. Make sure that your child is appropriately **dressed and equipped.**

4. Let the school know of your **concerns** and reinforce safety principles **at home.**

How to help your child
- [ ] Find out who is responsible for your child's safety.
- [ ] Find out what the school's safety requirements are.
- [ ] Contact the school if you are uncertain.
- [ ] Make sure your child is properly dressed.
- [ ] Find out what specialist equipment is needed.
- [ ] Talk to your child about safety.

Appeals

Key points

- Your right to appeal
- Different types of appeal procedure
- Matters for appeal
- Procedures to observe

While you may hope never to be in a situation of dispute with a school, it is as well to be aware of the various appeal procedures and where you should turn for help. Appeals against the decisions of a school or education authority may fall into one of four categories:

- appeals as part of the normal process of civil law
- appeals following legislative procedures established by Act of Parliament or the Secretary of State
- appeals to the local Commissioner or Ombudsman
- appeals through the hierarchy of the education system

Civil proceedings

Any matter involving the course needs specialist, technical advice. There are a number of situations where parents may wish to take an LEA to court, for example where all other procedures have failed. It is crucial to consult a **solicitor** and to obtain an estimate of costs — **legal aid** may be available in certain cases.

Appeals under legislation

Formal appeals procedures exist in three areas:

1. **Appeals against allocation to a school** — if you are not satisfied with the LEA's decision on which school your child should attend then you may appeal to a **panel.**

2. **Appeals against suspension** — you have a right of appeal to the **school governors** against a threat of suspension or an actual suspension. If you are not satisfied with their response (or with the mediation of the LEA) then you may appeal to the **Secretary of State**.

3. **Appeals against a Special Needs statement** — if you disagree with the assessment, and provision made in your child's case, then you may appeal to a panel set up under the **1980 Education Act**. If you are still dissatisfied then the right of appeal to the Secretary of State is available. (*See* the section, **Special Educational Needs,** on p.108 for an explanation of the Special Needs statement).

In all cases you should

- keep a **copy** of every letter you receive and send
- be absolutely **precise** about the facts leading to your appeal
- be clear about **how far** you are prepared to take your appeal and how much time, trouble and money you are prepared to invest in it
- remember that your appeal may **fail** and that your child will have to continue at school — avoid personal animosity.

Appeals to Commissioner or Ombudsman

The local Commissioner or Ombusdman has the power to investigate cases of maladministration, ie he can investigate the procedures of an LEA but not the *internal* affairs of a school. Thus you can appeal to the Ombudsman about the way in which an appeal was actually handled but not on the grounds of an appeal.

Appeals through the education hierarchy

Schools are part of a complex network of power and politics with a clear chain of responsibility. At each level individuals may overrule the decision of somebody lower down the chain. The pattern looks something like this:

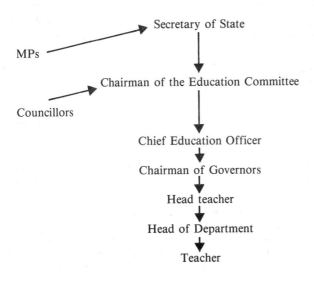

This is not a formal line of responsibility but it does show increasing *potential* to influence decisions. Two points must be borne in mind:

- **informal approaches** are more likely to work than demands and threats
- those in positions of power are likely publicly to **support their staff** — whatever they may say or do privately

Don't give up

Approaching elected representatives may produce results quickly if they are in a position to act. Members of Parliament have few *actual* powers to intervene in disputes between LEAs and parents; however their *influence* may be considerable and you could consider approaching your local MP if all else fails.

How to help your child

- ☐ Identify the correct procedure
- ☐ Obtain help and advice
- ☐ Keep careful and accurate records
- ☐ Keep your child's interests as your first priority
- ☐ Be persistent and make full use of the system

Examples of letters of Appeal

Allocation to school

I wish to appeal formally against the allocation of my daughter, Nicola Nickleby to Old Hall School. I wish her to attend Woodland Glade School which is the same school as her elder sister. Please let me know what the next stage of the procedure is.

Against suspension

My son, Harry Jones, was sent home from school for allegedly bullying Tom Smith. There are a number of matters which I wish to draw to your attention and I would be grateful for a meeting as soon as possible.

Against a special needs statement

I am writing to challenge formally the special needs statement concerning my child. I would be grateful if you could arrange a meeting with the appropriate education officer as soon as possible.

To the Chief Education Officer

I am writing to seek help with a problem at Albert Brown School. I am not satisfied with the standard of teaching in mathematics. The teacher does not seem able to keep control, work is not marked, and a lot of the resources are not being used. The headteacher insists that there is no problem. I am sending a copy of this letter to the headteacher, a parent governor and my local county councillor.

Attendance

Key points

- Parent's legal responsibilities
- Definitions of attendance
- Acceptable reasons for absence
- Alternatives to full-time attendance
- Contact with the school

Truancy is not the only reason for non-attendance, and parents need to understand the circumstances in which they may or may not keep their children away from school. In fact, parents have a legal duty to ensure that their children of compulsory school age receive efficient full-time education. **Compulsory school age** means:

- from the first day of the term following a child's fifth birthday
- to the first official leaving date after a child's sixteenth birthday

There are two official leaving dates:

1. the end of the Spring term for children born between 1st September and 31st January
2. the start of the Summer half-term holiday for all other children in their fifth year of secondary schooling.

A child who has remained at school after the official leaving date may leave at any time. Schools may require children taking exams to attend until the end of the examination period.

Full-time education

The dates of the school terms are decided by the LEA and governors. Children *must* attend in term time unless:

- the governors approve the absence
- they are ill
- they have to observe religious obligations
- the school is not within walking distance and no transport is provided (walking distance is 2 miles for children under eight, 3 miles for those over eight)
- parents are taking their annual holiday for a maximum of 2 weeks
- the headteacher has to close the school for any reason

Children may *not* be kept away from school:

- to look after younger brothers and sisters
- to care for a sick relative
- to work, except as part of a school organised scheme

In some circumstances children do not have to attend state schools:

- if they are in full-time attendance at an independent school
- if their parents are able to provide efficient education at home
- in the case of long-term hospital treatment
- if they have been placed in some form of institutional care

To prove attendance a child must have his or her presence in school recorded in the official **school register**. This means attending at times which are stated in the school handbook. Regular lateness is regarded as absence in another form.

The LEA has legal powers to enforce attendance — this is part of the responsibility of the **Educational Welfare Officer**. The best way to avoid confusion is to keep the school informed, preferably by letter:

Specimen letter

10 High Street
Anytown
1   9th October 1987

2 Dear Mr Brown

3 My son, Billy Bunter, has been absent from school for
4 four days with a stomach upset.

5 He has been placed on a special diet and will therefore be
coming home at dinnertime from now on.

Yours sincerely

6 . . . .

Notes
1   **Date** the letter.
2   Send it to the **teacher responsible for registering** your child.
3   **Identify** your child.
4   State the **period** of absence and the **reason**.
5   Indicate any **special factors**.
6   **Sign** the letter!

How to help your child

☐ Make sure you know when and where your child starts school
☐ Keep the school informed of reasons for absence
☐ Explain the legal requirements to your child
☐ Make sure you have details of holiday dates
☐ Obtain advice from the school or education office if you are uncertain

Bullying

Key points

- Bullying is not a normal part of school life
- Bullying can take a number of forms
- How to deal with bullying

Bullying is one of the oldest, most complex and intractable of school problems. It can cause profound distress, deep resentment and yet can be very difficult to control, let alone prevent.

The first major problem is to distinguish between youthful high spirits and horse-play, and deliberate malicious violence or intimidation. Youthful exuberance is one thing but any of the following, generally described as bullying, must be regarded as unacceptable:

- threats of violence
- demands for money, sweets, doing homework
- intimidation, such as preventing children using toilets
- provoking violence between children
- using actual violence

None of these activities can be condoned or excused. The problem is in deciding the appropriate response. There are a range of possibilities if your child complains of bullying. In the first instance believe your child. What can seem trivial to an adult may in fact totally dominate a child's life.

How to deal with bullying

1   Obtain as much **information** as possible about the bullying; names, dates, places and details.

2   Write to the appropriate teacher asking for an **investigation** and making an appointment for an **interview**.

3   It is highly unlikely that your child will be the only victim — the **more evidence** there is the better chance the school will have of resolving the problem.

4   **Trust the school** to take action in the first instance and let the staff decide on the appropriate sanctions.

5   If you are **not satisfied** with the school's response then you may contact the local education office or the school's governors.

6   In extreme cases you may choose to cooperate with the school in involving the **police** — inflicting physical violence and theft are criminal offences.

7   If the police are unwilling or unable to act then you have the option of a **private prosecution** — but you will need to obtain legal advice.

Take precautions
You can take certain steps to help prevent your child becoming a victim of bullying:

- never send them to school with more than the bare minimum of money
- don't let your son or daughter take expensive toys or personal effects to school
- encourage the formation of strong friendship groups to travel to and from school together, to spend break times together

In the final analysis no school has sufficient resources to *guarantee* a total absence of bullying. Equally no school can accept total responsibility for the behaviour of its pupils — home and community influences will inevitably predominate, for other parents' children as well as your own.

How to help your child

- [ ] Take any report of bullying seriously
- [ ] Involve the school as soon as possible
- [ ] Provide the school with as much information as you can
- [ ] Try to avoid making your child a target
- [ ] Believe your child

Careers Education

Key points

- Careers advice is a specialist activity
- Advice and skills
- Choices after school
- Realistic expectations

As a parent, the future employment prospects of your child will cause you concern, perhaps even anxiety, and it will help you to help your child if you understand how the school seeks to guide children in their choices.

Careers education is now established in most secondary schools. It will often be the responsibility of a specialist teacher or may be included in a pastoral care/personal development course.

The work of careers teachers is complementary to the work of the **Careers Service** which is run by the LEA and employs full-time **careers officers** who are concerned with providing guidance, information, helping organise the YTS scheme and links with employers.

The **Careers Department** in a school will not normally place school leavers in employment — its main functions are shown in the table:

The School Careers Department

1 Helps children understand the importance of making the most appropriate **career choice**;

2 Helps children understand the **requirements** of different types of work and how well they are **matched** to them;

3 Helps develop analytical skills to encourage effective **decision-making**;

4 Advises on appropriate **subject choices** for fourth and fifth year courses;

5 Advises on the **options** available after school;

6 Develops links with local industry, arranging visits, work experience and speakers;

7 Provides individual counselling;

8 Provides advice and guidance for parents.

This range of activities places a considerable demand upon the resources of a school and the skill and time of the careers staff. It is therefore in your interests to **seek advice** as early as possible and to play an active part in helping your son or daughter come to the best decision for them.

Two factors seriously limit the effectiveness of careers work:

● unrealistic parental hopes
● gender stereotyping

Beware wrong ambition

You will naturally want the best for your children but over-ambition can only lead to frustration and a sense of failure. The reverse is equally true — a child of intelligence and potential who is pushed into work below their capabilities is likely to react against it.

Knowing your child

To help your son or daughter make the best career decision ask yourself questions such as:

● Is she/he ready and willing to leave home?
● Does she/he enjoy studying and using books or more practical activities?
● What are her/his major hobbies and leisure interests?

Beware stereotyping

The idea of **equal opportunities** has been built into the curriculum of most schools but attitudes have not changed. There are still *girls'* subjects and jobs and *boys'* subjects and jobs. Parental attitudes can be crucial in supporting girls' genuine interests in science or engineering or boys' in nursing or catering.

Involve yourself

One of the most important elements in successful career choice is the active involvement, support and encouragement of parents. Informed advice needs to be supported by **family interest and involvement**.

How to help your child

☐ Give your support to careers education
☐ Attend careers interviews if at all possible
☐ Increase your own knowledge
☐ Be realistic but fully supportive
☐ Use contacts and friends as sources of information
☐ Encourage open discussion at home
☐ Check out a wide variety of options

Children in Trouble

Key points

- Police and school liaison
- Function of Juvenile courts
- Orders and appeals

If your son or daughter breaks the law then the education system plays an important part in the legal processes that follow.

The police

The head teacher has the same obligation to assist the police as any other member of the public. Equally he or she has an obligation to pupils and parents. If the police wish to interview a pupil in school then the teacher concerned may refuse to allow the interview to take place or let the child be taken to the police station until his or her parents have been informed. If this is not possible, or the child is willing to be interviewed, then **a teacher must be present**. If the police have a warrant then the head teacher must cooperate in its execution. The school may release a pupil's address to the police after consultation with the LEA.

Juvenile courts

Children (under the age of 14) and young persons (14 but not 17) who are charged with an offence are dealt with by juvenile courts.

If the case against a child is proved then the court will ask for a **report** from the education authority which will be prepared by the school. The report is designed to give the court as much information as possible about the child. Parents have a right to be told of any part of the report which deals with home matters and children to be told of anything relating to their conduct.

The report must be factual and objective and it may be discussed in court.

Juvenile court orders

The juvenile court can make a range of orders, some of which have implications for the school life of the child involved:

- a **supervision order** means that the court may require an offender to live in a particular place, to report to a specified individual or official or to take part in a range of activities. Such an order may include requirements about attendance and behaviour at school.
- a **care order** places the child or young person in the care of the local

authority. This may involve living in a community home which could mean changing school.

Appeals
A child or young person may appeal against a finding of guilt or an order of the juvenile court, or both, to the Crown Court.

School attendance
When an authority is satisfied that the attendance of a child is unsatisfactory then it may take a parent to court. If the court finds the case proved then it may impose a fine of £200 or a month's imprisonment or both if the offence is repeated.

Such an action may be accompanied by a care order to place the child in the care of the local authority, to ensure that he or she receives full-time education.

An authority may also issue a **School Attendance Order** requiring a parent to show that their child is receiving full-time education. Failure to respond to such an order may result in court action with the same penalties for non-attendance.

Seek advice
These procedures assume parental responsibility but you may find you are not able to control your son's or daughter's attendance. This does not lessen your responsibility and you remain **legally liable**. If you are aware of problems then contact the school and/or the Educational Welfare Officer.

Emotional problems
Changes in normal patterns of behaviour may well be the first clue that your child has problems and may be in some sort of trouble. Such changes might include: moody, withdrawn behaviour, changes in eating and sleeping habits, lethargy and apparently unexplained outbursts of anger and emotion. The crucial thing is to be more concerned with the cause than the symptoms.

How to help your child
- [ ] Be concerned, but don't make things worse
- [ ] Obtain professional advice
- [ ] Confront the problem not the person
- [ ] Look for alternative solutions
- [ ] Avoid turning a problem into problems.

Choosing A Primary School

Key points

- The right to choose
- Limits on choice
- Sources of information
- Making the best choice

For many people this will be their first introduction to the Education System — at least as an adult! Some understanding of what is involved will help you chart a course around the complexities.

The *1980 Education Act* gives parents a right to express a preference for the school that they wish their child to attend. However, in practice this right is often severely limited. The major restriction is the size of a school. Schools are staffed and receive resources according to the number of pupils on roll and the pupil — teacher ratio. These figures will vary but act as a ceiling on the number of pupils a head teacher can admit.

Practice varies but in most authorities priority will be given to children living within a school's **catchment area**. If there are vacancies then they are usually filled on a 'first come first served' basis. You will need to contact the head teacher well in advance of the term your child is due to start school.

LEAs can in some circumstances overrule parents' wishes but there is the right of appeal (see **Appeals**).

In some areas there is no real choice available, eg small rural communities. Where a choice is available then a number of factors need to be taken into account.

The Parents' handbook
This will give you basic information about the school but will also give an indication of how the school sees itself and what its principles are.

Local reputation
Talking to parents of children already at the school may well be your easiest source of information but beware of gossip.

Visit the school
This is the best way to make comparisons and come to a decision. Schools will vary enormously but certain factors are to be found in most good ones:

- Is your visit welcomed and are you given time to ask questions?
- Is the school relaxed and friendly?

- Is children's work displayed in classrooms and around the school?
- Are classrooms well organised from a child's point of view?
- Is there evidence of a range of resources and activities over and above normal classroom activities?
- Are parents regarded as 'partners' or outsiders?

Other factors
A number of other elements will play a part in your decision according to your views and your child's needs. These factors might include:

- the importance of religion in your life — Church schools will have close links with a particular religious viewpoint and way of life
- whether you favour a formal or informal approach to teaching (see **Curriculum — Primary**)
- your attitude towards uniform and discipline
- the distance of the school from home. Children build important friendships at school and it might be difficult to sustain these if a lot of travel is involved. Long journeys are not always the best way to start and finish the school day
- foreign language teaching and the use made of computers in the school
- the attitude towards sport and games
- the recognition of different social, religious and ethnic backgrounds of the local community

Exercise choice
Starting school is potentially very stressful for the five-year old. You know your child best and (within limitations) should choose the school that you *feel* is best. Your instincts are probably the clearest guide in deciding where your child will be happiest. When facing your choice, it might be helpful to consider the questions on the next page.

How to help your child

- ☐ Find out about the LEA's admissions policy
- ☐ Obtain a copy of the parents' handbook
- ☐ Visit the school
- ☐ Clarify your own views on what you expect for your child
- ☐ Assess what each school has to offer
- ☐ Analyse what is the best school for your son or daughter
- ☐ Talk about the decisions with your child

Finding Out about Primary Schools

Use these questions to build up a picture of a school:

1   How far is it from home? _____

2   Is the journey easy and safe? _____

3   Is it a church or county school? _____

4   Does it have school uniform? _____

5   How are classrooms organised? _____

_____

6   Is there plenty of children's work on display? _____

7   Is the prospectus clear and helpful? _____

8   How are computers used in the school? _____

9   What is the school's attitude to parents? _____

_____

10   What size are the classes? _____

11   How is progress recorded? _____

12   What are the arrangements for special needs? _____

_____

13   How are children supervised at break and lunch times? _____

14   What is the attitude to discipline? _____

_____

15   Does the school feel 'right' to you? _____

Choosing a Secondary School

Key points

- Stating a preference
- Limits on choice
- Obtaining information
- Making the best choice

As with primary schools the *1980 Education Act* gives parents a right to **state a preference** for the secondary school they would like their child to attend. However, the choice is even less real than it is for primary schooling. This is simply because there are far fewer secondary schools. In many areas there will be no choice; in some areas falling numbers mean school closures and mergers. Only in urban areas is there the possibility of choice.

Most LEAs will allocate final-year primary children to a comprehensive school or will ask parents to choose between a range of options with no guarantee of meeting the first choice.

If a choice does exist then the most important factor is finding a school that will have your confidence and support and in which your child will be happy and able to work effectively.

In making a choice you may be helped by:

- the school prospectus
- advice from the primary school
- visiting the new school
- local reputation

Read the school prospectus

This must provide you with information about how the school is organised, the curriculum and examination results. It will usually include details of the school day, school rules, clubs and organisations, discipline, and so on.

Take primary school advice

Your child's primary school will usually liaise closely with local secondary schools and your child's records will be forwarded to the appropriate school. It would be wrong to ask one teacher to pass judgment on another school but their knowledge of your child's ability and temperament may provide evidence for *you* to make a decision.

Visit the school

Secondary schools often organise open evenings for new children and their parents. How soon events are organised, their openness and frankness, will all provide you with a lot of informal information. If you want more information ask for an interview with the head teacher or (perhaps more appropriately) the teacher in charge of the first year.

Check local reputation
This is a difficult factor — the reputation of a school may be badly out of date and the product of local politics. The chances are that if the school 'feels' right to you then it is right.

Other factors
Secondary schools vary enormously — other factors which influence your choice might include:

- **Examination results** — important, but don't let them dominate; education is about far more than public examinations, however crucial they may be. A formal academic approach may not be best for your child.

- **Buildings** — paint and new furniture have been a low priority for several years — don't judge the quality of the school purely by its physical appearance.

- **Special characteristics** — single-sex and denominational schools are available in some areas; whether or not to send your child to such a school will depend upon your own attitudes and beliefs.

- **Facilities** — the range and quality of library, sporting, workshop and practical facilities will vary enormously. They may well represent the priorities of the school and this may help to develop your own view.

- **Size** — very small secondary schools may be cosy and friendly but lack the range of subjects; large schools will have excellent facilities but may be complex and impersonal.

- Your objective should be to find the school that comes closest to your ideal.

Be informed
Don't skimp on research. Take time to read the prospectus, take advice from the primary school and sound out local opinion. This can all be as worthwhile as visiting the school concerned. When carrying out your research, you might find it helpful to consider the questions on the next page.

Finding Out about Secondary Schools

Use these questions to build up a picture of a school:

1 How far is it from home? _____

2 Are the pupils grouped according to
   ability? If so, how? _____

3 How is the pastoral system organised? _____

4 What arrangements are there for communicating with parents? _____

5 What are the school's policies on
   uniform and discipline? _____

6 What range of subjects are available
   for examination courses? _____

   _____

7 Is the school mixed or single sex? _____

8 Is it a church or county school? _____

9 What are the facilities for technical
   subjects, computers and library
   resources? _____

   _____

10 What extra-curricular activities exist? _____

   _____

11 How is option choice in the 3rd year
    organised? _____

12 What provision is there for education
    after 16? _____

13 Does the school have a special reputa-
    tion in music, art or drama? _____

14 Does the prospectus give a positive im-
    age of the school? _____

15 Does the school feel right to you? _____

Choosing a School

Where a genuine choice does exist in choosing a primary or secondary school arrange the most important items *for you* in order of priority in the left-hand column. Then identify the key features of each school and set them against your preference.

	Topic	Your view	School A	School B
1				
2				
3				
4				
5				
6				
7				
8				
9				
10				

It should now be possible to identify the school that comes closest to your ideal.

How to help your child

☐ Find out about primary-secondary transfer arrangements
☐ Read the school prospectus
☐ Obtain advice from the primary school
☐ Visit the school
☐ List in order of priority what you expect from a school
☐ Talk about the decision with your child

Complaints

Key points

- Reasons for complaint
- Who is responsible?
- What is the best strategy?
- Procedures for making a complaint
- Principles to observe

There are numerous situations in the course of your child's education which might give rise to complaints. Many of these can be resolved quickly and simply by a letter or 'phone call to the school. Some may require a formal procedure (see **Appeals**), but there are many other areas which are not clear cut.

These include complaints about school policy, against individual teachers, victimisation or an unresolved dispute.

There are two important elements to consider in any dispute with a school:

- is the school, head teacher or individual teacher actually responsible?
- what is the best strategy to resolve the problem?

Complaints about teachers

Complaints about an individual teacher will almost certainly trigger a defence mechanism. A head teacher, colleagues, employer and teachers' unions will protect a teacher. You will not have the resources, time or expertise to challenge this. What you do have are rights as a parent and citizen which the education service will respond to if you present your case carefully.

- Obtain as much information as possible, eg if you are concerned about the lack of homework obtain a copy of the school's homework policy, find out what homework should be set and keep a record of how much is actually set.

- Write to the teacher concerned in the first instance asking for clarification.

- If you are not satisfied then ask for an appointment with the teacher concerned — at this stage a senior member of staff may well be involved.

- Work for an amiable settlement; anger (however justified) will only weaken your case.

- If you are unable to resolve the disagreement then you can write to the Chairman of Governors either at the school or the local education office (mark the envelope personal or confidential). Send a copy of the letter to a parent-governor and the Clerk to the Governors.

- If this fails then you may move your child to another school, follow the procedure outlined in Appeals, or widen your campaign.

It is important to remember that a teacher cannot be summarily sacked and disciplinary procedures are complex and drawn out. Such a procedure is unlikely to be initiated on the basis of one complaint.

If you believe your complaint to be sufficiently important then you can seek the advice of an organisation such as the **Advisory Centre for Education** or the **Children's Legal Centre**.

Their involvement may be enough to resolve the complaint. It is doubtful if letters to the local paper or petitions actually achieve anything except the hardening of attitudes.

Avoid aggression
The crucial thing is to find a solution that ensures that your child's education returns to normal as quickly as possible. Head teachers and teachers are no more likely to respond to anger and threats than you are. A dispute may disrupt your child's education, so the degree of action should reflect the importance of the complaint. Your willingness to negotiate will determine how quickly the dispute is settled.

How to help your child
- ☐ Find out the exact nature of the problem
- ☐ Establish who is actually responsible
- ☐ Choose the most appropriate strategy
- ☐ Adopt a positive, problem-solving approach
- ☐ Follow your complaint through
- ☐ Remember that reason will be more fruitful than anger

Curriculum — Primary

Key points

- Learning and teaching
- Balance of learning styles
- Balance of teaching methods
- How to be involved

The curriculum is not so much what children are **taught** as what they **learn**, and almost any positive activity can help learning. Crucial and central as they are, the '3 Rs' — reading, writing and arithmetic — should only be a *part* of school life and may be learned in a variety of ways.

There is no single 'right' way for children to learn. The crucial thing is balance — of learning styles, subjects and activities. Most schools will use a variety of methods, rote learning of tables or spellings balanced by creative writing and free expression in the arts.

The primary school curriculum is delivered in a number of ways:

- classroom organisation
- age grouping
- subject teaching

Classroom organisation

The way that a primary classroom is organised will tell you a lot about a school's **attitude** towards children. Lines of desks with the teacher at the front, children working on the same subject at the same time and a sense of regimentation will be familiar to many parents but is not necessarily the best or only way.

A modern classroom may well be organised in clusters of tables and activity areas, children working on a variety of activities and the teacher as guide and organiser rather than leader.

Neither approach is 'right' or 'wrong'; what is important is that it suits your child and that you feel able to support and show interest in the school.

Age grouping

As the numbers of children in primary schools have fallen so it has become difficult to maintain classes of children of roughly the same age.

Some schools adopt a deliberate policy of organising children into mixed-age **family groups** on the grounds that this is a 'natural' arrangement — older children can help the younger and brighter children are not held back. However, this arrangement requires special organisation by the teacher and fewer children in the class, but if it is forced upon a school then problems may arise, especially for younger or less able children.

Subject teaching

Although the primary curriculum will normally try and **integrate** distinct subjects, often using **project work**, certain subjects will be taught separately. These may include a modern language, usually French, science and perhaps technology (which may be known as CDT, Craft, Design, Technology). The ability of a school to offer these specialisms will depend upon the expertise of the staff and the resources and facilities provided by the LEA. If a small school loses specialist teachers, eg in music or languages, then it may be impossible to replace them, let alone their expertise.

Specialist teaching in some subjects such as music and French may be provided by **peripatetic teachers**. This does ensure that the subject is provided but obviously lacks the advantages of continuity and integration.

Be involved

The work of the primary school teacher may be supported in a number of ways:

- Getting to know your child's teacher, asking their advice and guidance.
- Setting time aside to talk to your child about their work.
- If possible, visiting libraries and museums but remembering that a bus, train or car ride or a visit to the shops can be just as educational if children are involved and encouraged to question.
- A set of encyclopaedias is no substitute for a few books which are shared and discussed.
- Watching television and playing with a computer can be positive if they are shared, discussed and explained.

There is no substitute for a parent's interest, support and involvement. Without it the school will never achieve as much as it could with it.

How to help your child

- ☐ Find out about the teaching and learning styles used
- ☐ Find out what specialist subject teaching is available
- ☐ Ask for further information if you are uncertain
- ☐ Involve yourself sympathetically in your child's work
- ☐ Reinforce the work of the school by activities at home

Curriculum — Secondary

Key points

- The five year secondary curriculum
- Balance of academic and non-academic
- Different learning styles
- Timetables
- Organising learning

The curriculum of the secondary school is, of necessity, in a state of continual change and development. The simplest definition of the curriculum is that it includes all activities that are provided for children in schools. Thus it is not just what is taught that makes up what a child learns. Visits, plays, school magazines and sports events are *all* part of the learning process.

The way in which academic studies are organised and taught has changed and will continue to change.

There are many new labels and names given to subjects or groups of subjects. One of the current priorities is that there should be a balance between the various subject areas. Ideally, the secondary curriculum should keep the following subject areas in balance for as long as possible:

Literacy	**Physical & Expressive**	**Non-Academic**
English Language Literature Modern Languages	Games PE Dance Drama Music	School Service Social Service Visits & Trips

Humanities	**Practical Studies**	**Science & Numeracy**
History Religious Education Geography Social Studies World Studies Integration Studies	Craft, Design & Technology Art Domestic Science Child Care	Mathematics General Science Physics Chemistry Biology Computer Studies

A school prospectus should indicate how these areas are interpreted and put into practice — one of your priorities in finding out about a new school should be to obtain a clear explanation of *what* is actually taught.

Teaching philosophy
How subjects are taught has also changed. Children do not necessarily learn effectively by listening to a teacher talking or copying down and learning facts. There is an increasing emphasis on children finding out for themselves, working in groups, undertaking projects and generally 'learning and doing'. Teaching styles vary enormously and there is no one 'right' way. What is essential is a balanced approach making use of a range of techniques so that children understand as well as learn.

Timetables
A school will deliver its curriculum through the timetable. Most comprehensive schools divide the working week into a number of periods (20, 30, 40 are common) and divide the subjects across the five days. Timetables are complex but certain principles should be followed.

- **Key subjects** — English, Maths, Science — should account for about 40%-50% of the total time.
- There should be a **balanced diet** for each day, eg Maths and Science, Art and CDT should not be consecutive.

One of the key issues for schools and parents is how **subject teaching groups** are organised. The range of methods includes streaming, setting, banding and mixed ability.

Streaming involves dividing children according to ability and then teaching them in classes which are of much the same ability. Children may be moved up or down but the classes remain distinct for all subjects.
Setting also involves dividing children into classes by ability but varying the sets according to the subject. Thus a child may be in Set A for Maths and Science lessons but Set C for English.

Banding is broad setting: a year may be divided into three or four bands by ability and the classes within each band are more or less the same.

Mixed ability means that no attempt is made to organise children into teaching groups by ability; instead each group is designed to have a cross-section of children from the most able to the slowest learner.

Schools will vary enormously in how they organise learning — mixed ability groups may be set for certain subjects, the first three years may be mixed ability, with banding and setting in years four and five. The research evidence is confused — able children do prosper under streaming but will often do equally well in mixed ability classes. Children who are late developers will be better off in banded or mixed ability types of organisations. Setting can cope with varying levels of interest and ability but can reinforce a sense of failure.

Look for quality
The crucial factor is not the method but the **quality** of teaching. The priority for parents is to find the system that will allow their child to develop.

How to help your child

- ☐ Obtain full details of subjects offered
- ☐ Find out how teaching is organised
- ☐ Look for balance in your child's timetable
- ☐ Ask teachers for information about subject content
- ☐ Obtain advice from the school if you are uncertain

Discrimination

Key points

- Laws on discrimination apply to schools
- Laws and attitudes
- Areas of concern
- Multi-cultural policies

The legislation which deals with discrimination on grounds of race, religion or gender apply as much to the education system as to any other aspect of life in Britain.

The education service has played an important role in working against discrimination but many problems still remain. The biggest problem is one of **attitudes** — of administrators, teachers, other parents and pupils. No amount of law-making will change attitudes but it can prevent the worst abuses and work towards the creation of a non-discriminatory climate.

The law relating to discrimination is complex; what follows is a general guide only:

Admission to school — it is unlawful for an LEA or head teacher to try and 'balance' the number of pupils in terms of race or gender.

Curriculum — pupils' choice of subjects should not be deliberately influenced by their race or sex.

Groups and clubs — no school organisation may limit its memberships on grounds of race or sex; obviously sports teams are based on merit, if this is clearly not the case then there are grounds for action.

Religious observance — parents are entitled to keep their children away from school to observe religious festivals.

School meals — where these are provided then some LEAs may make provision for religious and cultural dietary requirements, but they are not *obliged* to do so. If no provision is made then this is best pursued by a local pressure group but it is a matter for negotiation.

Uniform — where a school has a strict uniform policy then it cannot take priority over the law of the land. Patterns of dress which are required by cultural or religious observance, eg wearing the turban, not exposing limbs, should be respected by the school.

Schools are gradually evolving positive policies towards educating children to live in a multi-cultural society. However, they are constrained by resources and expertise. This is clearly an area for partnership between the school and local community, each working to improve its understanding of the other. Steps have been taken by LEAs, parents' and community associations; the best approach is one of openness and involvement, school and community making full use of each other.

Serious problems have arisen in schools with politically motivated attacks on racial groups. This might range from individual bullying to systematic intimidation and violence. In the final analysis such actions are illegal and warrant police involvement.

Schools can only respond to the needs of minority groups (of whatever type) if they know the needs of those groups. There is an equal responsibility to find out and make information available.

Coping with discrimination can involve a great deal of stress for the individual. Discrimination is an activity against the members of a group and therefore group action is often the best response.

The Citizens' Advice Bureau, library, legal centre, religious centre or community association will be able to help you or put you in touch with groups with the necessary experience and expertise. Some education authorities and schools have appointed specialist inspectors and teachers to deal with discrimination issues and they will be well placed to offer advice and suggest action.

The chances are that your problem is not unique and the experience and advice of others is your best starting point.

How to help your child

☐ Obtain advice from relevant organisations
☐ Make sure the school understands your special circumstances
☐ Become as actively involved in school life as you can
☐ Discuss potential problems with your child
☐ Use the law if all else fails

Examination Entry

Key Points

- Exam entry not automatic
- Factors influencing entry
- Payment of fees
- Types of examination

Entry to public examinations at the end of a child's fifth year at secondary school is *not*, and could not be, an automatic right. Not all children will reach the necessary levels of attainment to justify exam entry either because they do not have the necessary ability or because they have not done the work to have a chance of obtaining a pass grade.

A school's refusal to enter a child should not come as a shock to parents. The teaching group they are placed in for the fourth and fifth years, reports and parents' evenings should all indicate the likelihood of examination entry and potential success.

The GCSE is aimed at 60% of the fifth year population across the country. Therefore it is not suitable or appropriate for all children. In some schools more than 60% of fifth years will be entered, in some far less — this will depend, to some extent, on the social 'mix' of the school.

In the final analysis the decision to enter a child for any examination is one for the subject teacher in consultation with heads of department and the year head. Whilst exam entry might motivate some pupils, the possible impact of failure has to be taken into account.

Fees

If a school enters a pupil for an examination then the **examination fees** are paid by the LEA. Failure to take the examination without good cause *may* result in a demand for reimbursement of fees. Problems such as family bereavement or illness should be notified to the school as quickly as possible; they will advise you what action needs to be taken.

Exam boards

A variety of examinations are taken by pupils in their fifth year. Of these the most important is the **General Certificate of Secondary Education** (GCSE), examined for the first time in 1988 and administered by six regional boards. Other examination boards include the Royal Society of Arts, Pitman Examinations Institute and the City & Guilds of London Institute. You will find more information and their addresses in the section headed **Where to get help** on p.117.

It is worth remembering that all examination bodies publish booklets of their **syllabuses** and **rules and regulations** which are available to the public at nominal cost. These can be a means of seeing for yourself what the school and your child are undertaking.

GCSE

The GCSE replaces GCE O-levels and the CSE examination, the object being to simplify the examination process by having one examination.

Schools will normally take the examinations of the board in whose area they are geographically situated.

The examination boards will offer broadly parallel subjects although there may be some variations in the names given. There will be no difference in the standard of the examination between the boards.

The most important change is that instead of having to obtain a pass mark which is based on an estimated standard across the whole country **(norm referenced),** pupils will have to display their knowledge and understanding against a standard set by the boards *(criteria referenced).*

(*See* the section on p.60 for more detailed information about this examination.)

Royal Society of Arts

RSA examinations are most commonly met in commercial subjects, notably secretarial skills. These examinations are at three levels and are widely recognised by employers but need to be balanced by other qualifications. Much the same applies to **Pitman's** examinations.

City & Guilds

These courses are designed for pupils in their fifth year who wish to prepare for employment; there are nine broad areas of study available, eg food industries, community care and commercial studies. Each course is assessed and provides a basis for realistic career choices.

Putting your child first

Whatever form of assessment is considered the best interests of your son or daughter should come first — these may include *not* being entered for an examination or assessed course.

How to help your child

☐ Make a list of what courses lead to public examinations
☐ Find out details of the school's examination entry policy
☐ Monitor your child's progress regularly
☐ Check the school's exam entry timetable well in advance
☐ Make sure that your child is actually entered for the examinations

Examination Preparation

Key points

- Active preparation
- Planning and organisation
- Managing stress
- Support at home

Examinations are a regular feature of school life yet they remain a major source of stress. They are crucial to career prospects yet the mechanics of taking examinations are often ignored. This topic is dealt with in much more detail in another title in this series, *How to Pass Exams without Anxiety* by David Acres. All that is offered here are a few, very basic guidelines.

Examination preparation needs to be taken seriously and actively engaged in, not just learning the material to be examined but also considering how best to express it.

School (internal) exams deserve just as careful preparation as public examinations since they may well influence decisions about GCSE entry and they do play a part in forming teachers' opinions of children.

Reducing stress

Any examination period is a time of intellectual, physical and emotional stress and this can be alleviated by:

- being absolutely clear about **what** examinations are to be taken and **when**

- preparing an **examination timetable** which is prominently displayed at home so that everyone knows what is happening

- preparing a **revision timetable** which allocates time to each subject in such a way that each exam receives appropriate priority

- setting aside a **clear period** each day for revision

- remembering that **revision is an active process**. Aimless reading of notes is pointless; class notes need to be refined and reduced to manageable proportions using checklists, diagrams and self-testing

- being prepared to **listen, question and test**

- **controlling the time** spent revising — two hours of purposeful revision with clear objectives is better than four hours of aimless reading

Care at home

The examination period is long and demanding therefore:

- try to ensure that your child has enough **sleep** — revision into the early hours of the night before an exam is pointless and possibly damaging
- establish a **morning routine** so that there is plenty of time for breakfast and arrival at school in good time
- **encourage relaxation** — there is a place for watching TV, listening to records or going out with friends in any revision and exam timetable.

If the school has entered your son or daughter for an examination then they clearly believe that he/she has the ability to obtain an appropriate grade. There is no magic to passing — simply thorough and systematic revision carried out in a supportive and encouraging environment.

Support your child

Presents or rewards for passing are fine, and may even help to motivate in some circumstances, but they are no substitute for genuine interest and involvement.

How to help your child

- ☐ Obtain a copy of the examination timetable
- ☐ Help your child to plan the best use of time
- ☐ Be involved in revision
- ☐ Encourage a healthy and balanced lifestyle
- ☐ Be positive and supportive
- ☐ Try to keep a stress-free home environment
- ☐ Provide a quiet place for study at home

Extra-Curricular Activities

Key points

- Important but not compulsory
- The range of activities
- Factors for success
- Educational advantages

Extra-curricular activities are those aspects of the life of a school which are not formally timetabled or assessed but are seen as important elements of the educational process. Because they are not formal requirements the level of activity will depend on

- the interests and involvement of the staff
- the existence of resources
- the support of parents
- the commitment of children

Extra-curricular events will include a wide range of activities — visits, clubs, dramatic productions, foreign trips and so on. The level of such activities will be a major indication of the health and vitality of a school. However, they are, by definition, outside the normal teaching day and dependent upon the goodwill of teachers. Although there is an expectation that teachers will organise and participate in such activities there is no means of compulsion.

Involvement in clubs and societies is often seen as a crucial part of the broader educational process. They will provide opportunities for:

- developing good **personal relationships** between pupils and staff, helping staff to get to know children better

- enabling children to **accept responsibility**, manage activities and learn to work co-operatively and democratically

- encouraging the development of **knowledge and skills** which may not fit neatly into the formal curriculum

- helping children of **different ages and abilities** to meet so that they learn about and from each other

- recognising that life is about **more than academic learning** and that interests, hobbies and working with others are important aspects of the educational process.

Examples of the sorts of activities that may be found in schools include:

Sport
Many schools run teams in the major interest sports and competition with other schools is seen by many as a natural development of games lessons. Matches will often take place in the evenings and at weekends with coaching and training sessions at lunchtime or after school. Staff may also run after-school clubs on minority-interest sports — fencing, judo, squash and so on.

Clubs and societies
Many of these will arise naturally out of the curriculum. Music and art clubs extend and develop the work of those departments, computer and debating clubs will encourage interest and skills for which there is not time in the classroom.

Dramatic productions
For many schools these are the highlight of the extra-curricula year involving large number of pupils, staff and parents. The production of a play or musical involves much more than the acting of the 'stars', it will involve a wide range of skills (set construction, lighting, make-up, catering, publicity) which are of direct and indirect benefit to those involved. Acting ability may be the last thing to be developed compared with the discipline of working together, working to deadlines and producing a quality product for public performance.

Trips and visits
These are understandably one of the most popular forms of extra-curricular activity. They may arise directly out of the curriculum but take place in non-school time or in the holidays. The most common demand on parents in this respect is for money, but help in planning and supervision is often needed.

Parental involvement
With all these activities success depends upon voluntary involvement — of parents as much as students and staff. This involvement can take a number of forms:

● **Money** — because of their non-official status extra-curricular activities often have to be self-financing. This may involve a few pence for a club subscription to several hundred pounds for a foreign holiday.

● **Time** — the educational nature of these activities will often be enhanced by the involvement of parents giving their skills and knowledge to children.

- **Expertise** — a school's staff may not possess the full range of knowledge for all activities. Offers of help would normally be gratefully received but you should check on your position with regard to legal liability and insurance.

Supporting the school

Changing conditions of employment and industrial action have had a significant impact on extra-curricular activities and the pattern in future years too will change. However, the willing involvement and cooperation of parents can help to improve the range and quality of what is offered and at the same time help increase their understanding of what happens in schools.

Examples of extra-curricular activities

Art club	Sports clubs eg
Business enterprise group	— athletics
Chess club	— basketball
Community service	— cricket
Computer club	— football
Debating society	— gymnastics
Drama society	— netball
Go-karting club	— rugby
Model making club	— swimming
Music group	Stamp club
Natural history group	Visits and Trips
	Youth club

How to help your child

- ☐ Find out what activities are available
- ☐ Support them as an important part of school life
- ☐ Let the school know of any expertise you may be able to offer
- ☐ Be prepared to help with money and/or time
- ☐ Encourage your child to become involved
- ☐ Encourage your child to maintain a balance of interests

The General Certificate of Secondary Education

Key points
- Improving the old system
- Characteristics of the new examination
- Effects on teaching and assessment
- Changes in the content of courses

The GCSE is examined for the first time in 1988 and replaces the General Certificate of Education at O-level and the Certificate of Secondary Education. This change had been demanded for a considerable time because:

- it was often difficult to decide which exam to enter pupils for — the division was not always clear
- the CSE was never really accepted by employers or by further and higher education
- there was confusion as to the way in which the two sets of grades overlapped
- there was unnecessary duplication in the work of the exam boards
- it was increasingly felt that neither examination really reflected what children knew or had achieved.

From 1988 there is therefore the one examination at the end of the fifth year although the range of subjects will remain very much the same.

Main features of GCSE
The new examination has a number of significant features:

- it is based on **national criteria** for each subject, thus in theory there will be greater comparability between the examinations of different boards

- it will be **criteria** rather than norm **referenced,** ie children will pass at a level according to the level of knowledge they display rather than being fitted into a statistical average

- a significant proportion of the final exam grade will be based on **course work** done in school and assessed by the teacher

- the exam will be an opportunity to show **understanding** rather than a simple display of knowledge

- results will be **graded** on a seven point scale ABCDEFG with grade F as the performance of the average candidate. In theory at least there is no pass/fail but it seems almost inevitable that employers and other educational institutions will impose a 'pass' grade

- some exams will have **differentiated papers,** ie in order to qualify for certain grades candidates will have to take designated papers.

In practical terms GCSE will have an impact not only on the way in which courses are examined but also on what is taught and how. There will also be an inevitable knock-on effect on the curriculum in the first three years of the secondary school. A brief indication of the major changes can be gathered from the following 'basic' subjects.

English

The emphasis is upon learning to use the subject as a basis for effective communication. This means that spoken as well as written English is a part of the assessment process. Instead of students simply responding to a piece of reading they might, for example, be asked to

- retell a story
- explain it to a younger reader
- argue a case for or against
- describe emotions and moods

The skills of reading, writing, listening and speaking are thus used to develop skills of understanding, interpreting and communicating.

The same emphasis is applied to the study of literature where understanding and evaluating are coupled with the student's ability to communicate effectively.

Mathematics

As with English the aim of GCSE Maths is to develop understanding and the ability to communicate that understanding. Linked to this is the ability to understand mathematical concepts and to apply them through standard processes to practical problems. Equally important is the ability to interpret problems, identify the best way of solving them and then apply appropriate mathematical skills to the actual solution. Where possible such problems will be drawn from real-life situations.

Mathematics teaching will inevitably change with an emphasis on the use of practical materials, working in groups and discussion rather than the solitary completion of exercises.

Science

With science courses the shift in emphasis has been to the development of practical scientific skills and the application of knowledge. Thus the ability to *use* scientific processes is as important as the body of knowledge; equally significant is the application of that knowledge to social and economic issues and the problems and possibilities of science.

GCSE: Your questions answered

1 What's new about GCSE?

It is a single system of examinations, with a single scale of grades.

The examinations will test not only memory and orderly presentation of facts, but also understanding, practical and other skills, and the ability to apply knowledge.

All GCSE courses and examinations follow nationally agreed guidelines, known as 'national criteria'. These cover course objectives, content and assessment methods. The aim is to help pupils to benefit as much as possible from their studies.

The performance of candidates will be measured against defined yardsticks. 'Grade criteria' spell out what pupils need to know, understand and be able to do in order to achieve a particular grade in a subject. This means that pupils and teachers have clearer goals to aim at, and employers and colleges will have a much better idea of what candidates have achieved.

2 How is GCSE fair to candidates of differing abilities?

The new examinations are designed to demand more of able candidates than of less able candidates and to award grades accordingly. Within each subject there is a choice of papers or questions, which will give candidates of all abilities the opportunity to show what they understand, know and can do. Teachers will be able to guide pupils on which papers and questions to attempt.

3 How do GCSE grades compare with previous grades?

Successful candidates are awarded grades on a single scale from A to G. Grades A to C have standards at least as high as O-level grades A to C and CSE grade 1. Grades D to G have standards at least as high as CSE grades 2 to 5. Unsuccessful candidates will, as before, be ungraded and will not receive GCSE certificates.

4 Who is able to take GCSE?

Anyone, of any age, whether studying in a maintained school, an independent school, a further education college or privately.

5 How many subjects can a pupil take?

Pupils will be able, with the guidance of their teachers, to choose how many and which subjects to take at GCSE.

6 Is it possible to take GCSE in more than one sitting, or to resit GCSE examinations?

Yes, in both cases.

7 Are GCE A-levels or AS-levels affected by these changes?

No.

Adapted from *GCSE: The new exam system at 16-plus*, issued by the Central Office of Information.

Pupils will thus be required to devise and carry out experiments, being as concerned with the process and procedures of the experiment as with the actual outcome. Equally they will be expected to develop skills in problem solving, applying theory to practice and making decisions based on evidence.

The traditional subject areas of Physics, Chemistry and Biology remain but there are a number of courses catering for a cross-disciplinary approach, and these will increase in importance.

The central emphasis of all subjects is that the examination should allow and actually encourage students to show what they 'know, understand and can do'.

How to help your child

- ☐ Obtain information about the GCSE courses offered in school
- ☐ Get hold of syllabuses from the relevant exam board
- ☐ Attend briefing sessions run by the school
- ☐ Try to understand the new ideas in GCSE
- ☐ Look at your child's text-books and course work
- ☐ Discuss the courses with your child

Governors

Key points

- Composition of the governing body
- Governors powers and duties
- Potential influence

Every school maintained by an LEA has a body of governors. The membership is made up of three elements: parents, teachers and representatives of the LEA and local community. The precise duties and powers of a governing body will vary from one LEA to another; equally the ability of governors to influence a school will depend upon their relationship with the head teacher.

Parent and teacher governors are **elected**, others **appointed** by the LEA. The only qualification to be a parent-governor is simply to be a parent of a child in the school. There are no political requirements.

The names of the governors of a school will normally be found in the school prospectus, though means of contacting governors are not always shown — a letter to the Chairman at the school will be forwarded.

Governors' duties

Governors have a range of duties:

- oversight of the curriculum but not textbooks or teaching methods
- joining in decisions on matters of school finance
- the appointment and dismissal of the head, teaching and non-teaching staff
- agreeing school holidays and hours
- confirming the suspension and reinstatement of pupils
- deciding the way in which sex education should be taught

Head teachers present regular reports to governors outlining important developments in the school. Governors prepare an **annual report** for parents and hold an annual **open meeting**.

Governors have little formal power but a great deal of potential influence. The best relationship is one of mutual respect and partnership in which governors work with parents and teachers to support and develop the school.

In the event of a dispute governors can act as mediators but they cannot act as judge or jury. The precise powers of governing bodies are laid down by each LEA and you should be able to obtain a copy of the 'articles' from education offices.

Ideally governors will act as a link between the school and parents and the wider community. Parent-governors in particular are well placed to raise worries and doubts and to pass on reassurances and information.

Effective governors need to undertake **training** through courses organised by the LEA, local colleges, The Open University or the National Association of Governors.

Parent Governors

In order to become a parent governor you will need to take part in an election. The school will normally announce the date of an election and invite nominations. You will need to complete a nomination form, have it signed by nominating parents and return it to the school. You will also have an opportunity to send a statement to all parents describing your background, past involvement in the school and areas of expertise and interest.

Once elected you will have to attend regular meetings of the governing body and equally importantly become involved in the school. This might be done by taking a special interest in an aspect of the school's work, visiting the school and attending school functions, being available to other parents and supporting the school in the community.

How to help your child

☐ Find out who the parent governors are
☐ Attend the annual open meeting
☐ Consider becoming a governor yourself
☐ Use the governors as a source of information and advice

Grants

Key points

- Education is free but can involve extra expense
- Mandatory and discretionary grants
- Types of assistance

State education in Britain is **free**. There is no charge for tuition, textbooks or basic facilities. However, it would be ridiculous to pretend that all facilities are equally available to all children. Much of the quality of education does depend upon extra resources for practical lessons, trips and visits, sports equipment and at a more basic level uniform and shoes.

LEAs can make two types of grant:

- **mandatory** — they *must* be paid to eligible cases
- **discretionary** — they *may* be paid to eligible cases

Precise details as to what grants are available and how to apply for them should be available from your LEA; your child's school or the Education Welfare Officer may be able to help. Equally the Citizens Advice Bureau or Social Services will be able to offer advice. The Child Poverty Action Group and Gingerbread will also be able to help (see addresses on p.117).

Grant applications

Applying for any educational grant is a complicated matter. The forms are very detailed and often confusing. They will almost always require exact details of your family and financial circumstances.

Educational grants are **means tested** — the amount of grant payable will be related to your net income, ie the sum left after expenses — such as mortgage or rent, allowances for other children, the cost of getting to work — have been deducted from the total income.

Mandatory grants

Examples of mandatory grants include:

- **Travel** to and from school if the distance involved is more than two miles for primary age children or three for secondary pupils. Costs may be met by providing buses or taxis or issuing bus passes.

- **School meals** — are free if family income is below a level set by the DES. However, they have to be applied for annually. (Schools should develop systems which do not identify children receiving such meals.)

- **Boarding education** must be provided if there is no alternative way of providing a suitable education.

Discretionary grants
Discretionary grants include:

- Money towards the costs of **school uniform**. This is highly variable and causes considerable difficulty as there is no agreement as to what constitutes a uniform. Some LEAs will provide cash, some vouchers and others will reimburse parents. Shoes and winter clothing may be included — information about what is available may be obtained from Educational Welfare Officers. Clothing for PE and games may also be provided.
- Assistance may be available to help children join **clubs and societies** and to take part in **journeys** and **field trips** which are a necessary part of the curriculum.
- LEAs have the legal powers to make special payments to encourage the development of **special talents**, eg in music, dance or art. Similarly there may be special trust funds set up to help with certain aspects of education.

However, discretionary payments are inevitably an early casualty of government cutbacks and in many areas there may simply be no money available.

How to get help
To find out about what grants are available contact the school first; if they cannot help then contact the Area Education Office or Education Welfare Officers.

How to help your child
- ☐ Obtain advice on what grants are available
- ☐ Check your entitlement
- ☐ Do apply if you are eligible
- ☐ Be aware of the potential for embarrassment or disappointment!

Homework

Key points

- Homework as an integral part of school work
- Setting up routines
- How to help

A school's policy on homework should be clearly stated in the *Parents' Handbook*. Homework does make a difference if it is used as part of an overall teaching strategy and not a means of carrying out routine tasks such as completing unfinished work.

Homework is a means of developing individual study skills, providing children with the responsibility for their own learning and providing an important link between home and school.

Primary school children are rarely set formal or systematic homework although help with reading is always relevant and appropriate. More explicit or formal help is best discussed with your child's teacher.

Secondary school homework

In most secondary schools homework is set on a regular basis:

- the **amount set** will vary from about 30 minutes per evening in the first year to 2 hours in the fourth and fifth years

- your child should be given a **homework timetable** showing what subjects are due on what evenings

- there should be a **homework record book** which indicates clearly what is expected and by when

Helping with homework

Homework will only be taken seriously and done effectively if:

- it is given a **high priority** in domestic routines

- **space** is provided free from distractions with a desk or table, proper lighting and quiet

- a **regular time** is established which sets homework in the context of television watching and meal times

Homework can create considerable anxiety and domestic stress. The major question for parents is often how much help to give, if indeed they are to help. Problems in science and mathematics will often be outside your experience. The crucial thing to remember is that parents should *not* attempt to do the homework but rather help their child to understand and complete the work themselves.

This may be done in a number of ways:

- maintain an **active interest** in what is happening in your child's lessons
- **read through** your child's exercise books, asking for clarification and explanation
- get to know the **textbooks** if they are available
- be **available** to help

Lack of understanding will often be the major problem — the following stages may help to clarify what is required:

- Is the assignment title clearly understood?

- Is the work done in school on which the homework is based available and understood?

- Get your child to teach *you* the subject; work together to ensure understanding; ask questions rather than give answers.

- Go through the finished work (done in rough) asking for explanations and clarification.

If there is still a problem let the teacher know. Homework marks are often an important part of **assessment procedures** and problems need to be remedied quickly.

Don't do it for them!
Support your child by all means, but there is no point in actually doing your child's homework; a properly organised homework schedule is designed to help learning which is an *individual* process.

How to help your child

- ☐ Find out the school's policy on homework
- ☐ Provide a suitable environment at home
- ☐ Establish a regular domestic routine
- ☐ Involve yourself in the work, but don't do it
- ☐ Ask the school for information about its place in the course

Independent Schools

'Independent schools' is a general term used to describe those schools which are not financed or administered by Local Education Authorities. The crucial difference between independent and state schools is that independent schools charge **fees** which they set themselves.

There are a wide range of independent schools; they may be broadly classified as follows:

- **Public Schools** These are usually long established and the head teacher will be a member of the Headmasters Conference — an indication of established reputation. These schools are usually, but not always, boarding schools.

- **Private Schools** This term covers a very wide range of schools including the former direct grant grammar schools which became independent in the 1970s.

- **Free Schools** are very few in number and are generally 'progressive' in nature, adopting a less formal approach to education.

The independent sector caters for the full age range of children from pre-school to sixth-form. One way in which it differs significantly from the state system is in the age structure of independent schools, many of which work on the ages of 8-13 for preparatory schools and 13-18 for public schools. Transition from one phase to another is by the **Common Entrance Examination** which is highly academic and competitive.

One of the strengths of the independent sector is the wide **choice** of educational environments available. Almost all religious denominations are represented in the independent sector. Similarly there is a choice of boarding or day, single or mixed sex, traditional or progressive. A number of independent schools specialise in the education of physically or mentally handicapped children or those with problems in adjusting to 'normal' schools.

Fees
Independent education is expensive — fees vary enormously, from several hundred pounds for a place at a day school to several thousand at the

most prestigious boarding schools. Several schemes are available to help with fees:

- **Scholarships** Many schools offer a limited number of places which carry remission of fees; these are usually competitive and based on academic ability.

- **Subsidies** These are usually found in cathedral schools where the fees of choristers will be reduced.

- **Assisted Places** This is a government scheme to help parents meet the cost of private day education.

- **LEA Funding** LEAs have limited discretion to pay the fees of children at independent schools, for example in the case of exceptional musical talent or special medical needs. However, this is a very limited source of funding.

Your choice — independent or state schooling?

In the final analysis this choice depends upon your ability to pay. Only seven percent of children attend independent schools and the choice does not exist at all for the majority.

For many parents the choice will also be a political one — whether or not they believe in the principle of fee-paying education.

If the decision is made to send a child to an independent school then the choice is considerable. The same principles of choosing a school apply as with state schools. It is important to note that a school which is registered with the DES simply conforms to certain basic standards of resources and facilities. A better guide is schools which are recognised as **efficient** by the DES, which means they have been inspected.

There are a number of private consultancies offering advice on the choice of independent schools but the best source of information is The Independent Schools Information Service, 56 Buckingham Gate, London SW1E 6AH (Tel: (01) 630 8793).

How to help your child

- ☐ Would your child really benefit? — make a list of pros and cons
- ☐ Check the advantages of independent over state education
- ☐ Discuss the issues fully with your son or daughter
- ☐ Check out all the costs in detail
- ☐ Be sure you are putting your child's interests first

Inspectors and Inspections

Key points

- Local and national inspectors
- Local advisers
- Powers and duties
- Limits to their authority

Inspectors have a vital role in education today and it is well for a parent to understand what their responsibilities and powers are.

There are two categories of inspectors in the education service, those appointed by Local Education Authorities (who may also be known as **advisers)** and **Her Majesty's Inspectorate** (HMI). They are quite distinct groups and work in very different ways although they share the same basic concern — the quality of education.

LEA advisers and inspectors

LEAs have the power to appoint inspectors but there is no ruling about how many or what their functions are. They will normally have three areas of responsibility: for a subject area; for a sector of education (primary, secondary etc); for managing aspects of an LEA's work.

Functions

There is no real difference in the functions of advisers and inspectors; advisers inspect, and inspectors advise. Their main functions are:

- advising on the promotion and appointment of teaching staff
- organising and delivering in-service training for teachers
- inspecting and reporting on the work of individual schools
- advising on good practice in teaching and management of schools
- acting as a link between schools and the local education authority and its officers

Parents have no general right of access to the LEA inspectorate. Normally they would only meet as the result of a **complaint** or **appeals procedure.** A letter to a Chief Education Officer about an individual school or a curriculum issue will probably be replied to by the appropriate inspector.

Inspectors are a useful source of information about LEA policies on a wide range of matters, but they do not have the time or resources to act as an information service.

Her Majesty's Inspectorate

HMI are an independent group of senior and experienced educationalists who are appointed by the Queen. Although accountable to the Secretary of State they see their first loyalty as being to the education service and not the government of the day. There are about 500 HMI and they are regionally organised into teams of **subject** and **sector** specialists.

The work of HMI may be divided into three aspects: developing, inspecting and reporting.

Developing
HMI are a major source of new ideas in education. In recent years they have been particularly responsible for much of the work in developing new initiatives about the curriculum and the management of the teaching service.

Inspecting
HMI have the right to inspect any educational institution and this is a major aspect of their work. Since 1982 **reports** on individual schools and colleges have been published. These reports often represent the only detailed public source of information about a school (although only a minority of schools have actually been inspected). If an HMI report is available on a school to which you are thinking of sending your child then a number of points need to be borne in mind:

● the report will be an historical document: often reports are not published until 18 months after the inspection
● it will be based on a visit of 5-10 working days and so is a 'snapshot' of the school
● HMI have no power to force change on a school nor have they any control over resources or money
● HMI reports are detailed and technical; beware of sensational extracts in the local press which may well give a biased view of the school.

Reporting
A major function of HMI is to report to the Secretary of State on the condition of education in England and Wales. One of the most important of these reports is an annual commentary on the impact of economic cuts.

HMI have great influence but little direct power. Their publications and reports can provide parents with a great deal of invaluable information on current educational thinking and problems. Reports on individual schools are available from LEAs; other HMI publications are available from: Department of Education and Science, Elizabeth House, York Road, London SE1 7PH. (Tel: (01) 934 9000).

Medical Matters

The development of the education service has seen a parallel growth in the work of the **School Health Service**. Although the School Health Service does much of its work in schools it is not a part of the education system but is run by the local health authority.

The School Health provides a range of inspections which includes:

- **medical inspections**, which are compulsory and normally take place at the ages of about 5, 12 and 15 years. Parents have a right to be informed about the inspection and present if they wish. An important part of this process is the medical record card which remains with the child throughout their school career.

- **Eyesight tests** are a simple screening process and will usually involve referral to a doctor or optician if there is a problem. Testing for colour blindness is particularly important as it may have safety and career implications.

- **Hearing tests** are obviously crucial — many children have been wrongly classified as being slow or backward when in fact they suffered slight hearing loss.

- **Inspections of hair and feet** are caried out regularly and parents will be advised if any action is necessary. Head lice are a common problem, are easily dealt with and should involve no social disgrace.

The School Health Service will organise BCG and Rubella vaccinations which provide immunity against TB and German measles although parents may organise them through their own GP.

Your child and diseases

Schools are obviously places where infectious diseases can spread very easily. It is therefore essential to observe medical guidelines as to when it is safe to let your child return to school. Your GP or community physician will advise what diseases require specific periods away from school.

If your child is in contact with diphtheria, polio, smallpox, tuberculosis or typhoid then they must not be sent to school. Similarly the school should be informed of a case of German measles because of the danger to pregnant women.

Other problems

Children are subject to a wide range of medical problems, many of which can interfere with learning or happiness at school. The crucial thing is to let the school know what the problem is, how it affects your child and what help, if any, is needed from the school.

It is particularly important to let the school know if your child is following a course of treatment. Younger children should not be allowed to carry medicines around with them at school. Only sufficient dosage for the day should be sent to school and left in the safekeeping of the appropriate member of staff.

Certain medical conditions can lead to considerable social problems for children. Acne or eczema, speech impediments and obesity can all cause distress and lead to anti-social attitudes. Discussions with teachers and your own GP may help, but if need be seek specialist advice.

Educational psychologists are able to offer diagnostic help and develop programmes of treatment. However, the demand for their services far outstrips the supply. Schools will normally refer children to an educational psychologist and should consult parents in advance.

Psychologists can help with problems such as school phobia, diagnosing dyslexia, managing the hyperactive child and identifying learning difficulties.

However, no amount of professional help can really succeed without the full involvement of parents.

How to help your child

☐ Keep the school fully informed about health matters
☐ Accompany your child to medical inspections if at all possible
☐ Seek specialist advice when necessary
☐ Tell the school about any medication your child needs to take during the day

Options — Fourth Year

Key points

- Subject choice for fourth and fifth year courses
- Stages in the decision-making process
- Factors influencing choice
- Care and optional subjects

At some point during the third year of secondary education children are asked to choose their subjects for study in the fourth and fifth years, in effect choosing courses that may lead to public examinations. This is a crucial process as academic success and employment prospects will be very largely determined by the choices made.

The stages of choice

The process of option choice will usually include the following stages:

- **Examinations** — the results, with classwork, will help to indicate strengths and weaknesses and so provide a basis for sensible subject choices.

- **An options brochure** — this should outline the procedures for choosing subjects, give information on the subjects available and show what combinations are possible.

- **Careers advice** — the school's careers staff may run lessons helping children identify their strengths and weaknesses and main interests, and working out the implications for subject choice of career intentions.

- **Parents' evenings** — a chance for parents to discuss the options with teaching staff and discuss their child's potential in order to help in making a realistic decision.

- **Counselling** — by pastoral and careers staff to help with individual questions.

- **The actual choice** — which will usually be made on a pro forma which parents may be asked to counter-sign.

Factors of choice

Certain key factors need to be taken into account in choosing subjects:

- **Ability** — the advice of teachers is crucial if children are to make the most of their courses. Not all children are capable of taking public examinations and equally parents should not attempt to limit their children. Over and under ambition can lead to boredom and frustration.

- **Career needs** — most employers and further education establishments now have quite clear and precise entry requirements and these must be taken into account.

- **Favourites** — however tempting it may be, children should be dissuaded from making choices purely on the basis of liking a particular teacher or subject. Both will change during examination courses.

- **Gender** — girls in particular need guidance to avoid opting for girls' subjects, notably at the expense of science and technology subjects.

Subject choices
The range of subject choices available for fourth and fifth year courses will vary from school to school. Some may only offer two or three choices, some as many as seven. Most will insist upon a number of core subjects — English Language, Mathematics, RE and PE/Games.

There may then be a totally open choice or, more likely, choices of one subject from a limited range, structured in such a way as to ensure a range of subjects covering the main elements of the curriculum. A typical scheme might look like this:

Physics	History	Chemistry	CDT
Chemistry	Geography	French	Art
Biology	Social Studies	Typing	German
General Science	Biology	Childcare	Domestic Science

A major constraint is often the size of groups — there will be a limit to the number of work places in laboratories and workshops. Therefore compromise may at times be necessary; if this is not possible then be prepared to negotiate with the appropriate head of year, deputy head or head teacher.

Laying foundations

The central aim of option choice is to lay foundations for educational and career development whilst allowing for changes of mind.

How to help your child

☐ Attend open and parents' evenings
☐ Read the options booklet
☐ Seek advice and clarification if necessary
☐ Discuss the options in detail with your child

"Perhaps I should drop chemistry!"

Fourth Year Options

Do you know:

1 What subjects are compulsory in the fourth year?

2 What options are available?

3 Are any combinations of subjects impossible?

4 Are any combinations of subjects obligatory?

5 Is there a requirement to take categories of subject
   (ie 1 science, 1 humanity, 1 craft)?

6 What subjects are your son or daughter likely to be entered
   for in GCSE?

7 What subjects are they unlikely to be entered for?

8 What are your son's or daughter's favourite subjects?

9 Are there any subject requirements for their chosen career
   or job?

10 What choices do the teaching staff suggest?

Options at Sixteen

Key points

- The options available
- Factors influencing choice
- Continuing education or employment
- Academic or vocational education
- School or college

At the end of their fifth year most school leavers are faced with a range of choices:

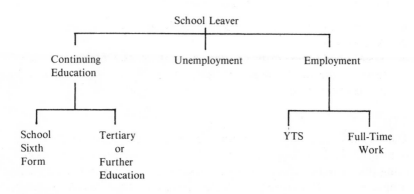

It would be wrong to pretend that the choice is equally real for all school leavers. A number of factors need to be considered:

- **Ability** — how far does your son or daughter wish to pursue an examination-based, academic career?

- **Aptitude** — what are their interests and abilities and how will they be best served?

- **Finance** — education remains free but living expenses are high.

Such decisions are crucial and need the maximum amount of advice from teachers, careers staff and the Careers Service.

Sixth forms
Options available will include:

- Repeating **fifth year exam** failures, rarely as successful as is hoped and a year is lost.

- **Certificate of Pre-vocational Education** (CPVE) courses designed to link school and work with an examination content appropriate to the individual.

- **Advanced level GCEs** which are the basis of higher education; specialist advice is essential for A-level subject choice.

Tertiary and Further Education Colleges
These vary enormously in size and range of courses. Tertiary colleges may be sixth form colleges or combine the full range of further education courses. The range will normally include:

- CPVE/City & Guilds foundation courses
- A-levels
- Vocationally-orientated courses concentrating on training and education for the whole range of employment, from basic level to pre-university courses.

YTS
The Youth Training Scheme is a genuine alternative to continuing education in school or college for all ability levels. Many industries are now using it as a replacement for the apprenticeship system and a very high proportion of YTS trainees obtain full-time employment. Work experience has to be accompanied by training and the two-year scheme offers many young people a coherent preparation for work.

Employment
There are jobs available for 16-year-old school leavers which may well offer apparently high rates of pay and if it is a matter of a job at any price then any cautionary advice is bound to be of limited use. But the crucial questions to ask are what *training* is provided and does the pay reflect *age* and *experience*? If the answer to both is no, then the job is little more than cheap labour which, when considering future employment prospects, may not even serve as a basis for competition with YTS and college trained students.

Unemployment
With the extension of the YTS, unemployment ought not to be an option for the 16-year-old. Refusal of a YTS place or course at school or college

only serves to increase the possibility of long-term unemployment. The lack of any form of qualification or experience, combined with the extra competition of the next group of school leavers, makes life increasingly difficult for the young unemployed.

How to help your child

☐ Discuss long term ambitions and plans
☐ Identify realistic alternatives
☐ Obtain plenty of advice from the school and careers office
☐ Discuss options fully with your son or daughter
☐ Collect as much printed information as possible

Sixth Form Options

Do you know:

1 What subjects are available in the sixth form?

2 Are there more appropriate courses/qualifications at a college of further education?

3 What is the best environment for your son or daughter?

4 What are the entry requirements for his or her chosen course or career?

5 Are there any conditions for entry to particular subjects?

6 Do some subjects have to be taken in combination?

7 What arrangements are there for retaking subjects failed in the fifth year?

8 What is the advice of the subject teachers and career advisers?

9 Is the time in the sixth form likely to be more profitable than a YTS scheme or vocational training?

10 Does your son or daughter really want to continue in full-time education?

Parents' Associations

Many schools have established organisational links between parents and the school, usually aiming to:

- **improve communication** between home and school
- help to **channel the views of parents** to the local community, LEA and central government
- organise **special events**
- **raise funds** for special projects, equipment, trips and visits

How such a group is established and how it works with the school is very much the head teacher's decision. Indeed, a head could actually refuse to have such an association.

Status of parents' associations

Confusion sometimes arises about the status of parents' associations:

- there is no requirement that they should actually exist

- they have no right to use school buildings or resources

- they have no part to play in the internal management or government of the school — that is the responsibility of parent-governors

- the head teacher has the right to decide what equipment/resources the school needs and how best to utilise such things

In practice these problems will not occur if there is a willingness on both sides to negotiate. It is worth remembering that voluntary activities for parents may well be unpaid overtime for teachers and their goodwill and involvement should not be assumed.

Forming new associations

If no association exists then a number of crucial questions need to be asked at the outset:

- What is the primary purpose in setting up an association?

- What is the attitude of the head teacher and staff?

- How is the association going to be organised?

- What is the membership to be? Parents only, parents and teachers or any interested members of the local community?

Well organised parents' associations can do much to enhance the quality of life in a school if they:

- respond to the stated needs of the school

- publicly work to develop the image and reputation of the school

- avoid becoming a clique of a few parents excluding, however unintentionally, the majority

The best approach for an association is one of supportive partnership.

Advice on setting up and running a parents' association can be obtained from the **National Confederation of Parent-Teacher Associations** (*see* **Where to Get Help**).

How to help your child

- ☐ Become actively involved — social contacts are more important than fund raising
- ☐ Work in partnership with the school
- ☐ Recognise the limits on the activities of PTAs.
- ☐ Obtain advice from the National Confederation
- ☐ Enjoy your participation!

"What can we do about these apathetic parents of ours?"

Pastoral Care

Key points

- Social and academic development
- Pastoral systems
- Functions of pastoral staff
- Guidance and administration

There is a long tradition in British schools that teachers have a responsibility for the well-being and personal development of pupils as well as teaching academic subjects. This aspect of the work of schools is often referred to as pastoral care.

In **primary schools** pastoral care is very much built into the work of the class teacher and, when necessary, the head teacher. **Secondary schools** have developed complex structures to achieve the same result.

Whose responsibility?

Pastoral care in secondary schools is, in general terms, the responsibility of all staff but a number of specialists will be appointed.

- The **deputy head teacher** (pastoral) will be the senior member of staff responsible for the overall well-being and discipline of pupils.

- **Heads of year** or **heads of house** are responsible for groups of pupils organised by year (ie age) or in vertical groupings (mixed age).

- **Form tutors** will have day-to-day contact with pupils.

All of these teachers will have teaching responsibilities and varying amounts of (usually very limited) time to deal with pastoral matters.

The work of pastoral staff may be divided into two broad categories as shown on the opposite page.

The range of responsibilities will vary from school to school and it is usually the case that the more serious the problem the more senior the staff who deal with it. Some schools give a great deal of responsibility to the form tutor — others limit responsibilities to senior staff. Whom to contact and how to contact them should be shown in the school prospectus or handbook.

The school can only help your son or daughter if they have up-to-date and accurate information which is relevant to their work and progress.

Confidentiality

This raises a problem of confidentiality in that information needs to be circulated to all your child's teachers if it is to be taken into account. It

Functions of pastoral staff

Personal	Administrative
Guidance and counselling of pupils with problems	Liaison with social services, educational welfare officers, the police, juvenile courts
Individual discipline	Organising parents' evenings
Careers and options guidance	Keeping records of progress and attendance
Sorting out individual worries and difficulties	Liaising with parents
	Organising option choices

is up to you to discuss with the pastoral staff who needs to know and how much. A visit to the school is the best way to pass on sensitive information.

Contact and help

Pastoral staff are not permanently available — they have to teach, attend meetings and undertake a wide range of duties. To be sure of having the time that you need with the appropriate teacher always try to make an appointment. Help will be offered if at all possible but teachers are not social workers, doctors or marriage guidance counsellors.

Schools have wide experience of dealing with the full range of the problems of childhood and adolescence. Larger schools may have a professionally qualified counsellor able to help or suggest other sources of help.

How to help your child

☐ Find out how the pastoral system works
☐ Obtain the names of pastoral staff and get to know them
☐ Use the liaison procedures established by the school
☐ Make full use of the expertise and advice available
☐ Keep a sense of perspective — hard at times!

Pre-school education

Key points

- Preparing for school
- Playgroup or babysitting?
- Appropriate activities
- Learning in the family

Starting school is potentially stressful for child and parent alike, and there is much that can be done to make the process easier. An important part of this process can be the **playgroup** or **nursery school**. Although playgroups are not schools and their staff are not teachers as such, they can have a role to play in helping to prepare children for school itself. The same can be said of nursery schools, where the educational content can be expected to be greater, and the staff more qualified.

Choosing a playgroup
Two simple checks should be applied to a playgroup:

- Has it been **inspected** by the social services department to make sure that the accommodation is appropriate and safe and that there are enough adults?

- Is it linked to the **Pre-School Playgroups Association**, eg have the staff followed one of its training courses?

Choosing a nursery school
Nursery schools have a more structured, educational basis, but they are scarcer and places are more limited. If you choose nursery education for your child, then find out the admission procedure at an early stage and reserve a place well in advance.

Rising fives
In some schools there is a policy of admitting children before their fifth birthday — sometimes known as 'rising fives'. This depends upon LEA policy and the space available in the school. You may ask the head teacher about the possibility of early admission but it is not an automatic right and depends upon local circumstances.

Preparing for school
Playgroups and nursery schools can be considered an extension of the process — which should be centred on family life and the home — of preparing a child for school. There can be no hard and fast rules about what

a child needs in order to make a successful start in primary school. Pre-school groups can help to teach and foster those skills which will assist in making the transition easier, skills which are both social and educational:

- **Practical skills** like managing at meals, dressing and fastening shoes, using the toilet and washing, being able to ask clearly for help
- Learning to **work in groups,** to cooperate and share with other children
- Learning to **listen**
- Learning to **play and work individually**
- Playing in a **positive, creative and purposeful** way
- **Experiencing** music, paint, modelling and puzzles
- **Talking** with adults and peer group
- Learning to **cooperate** in routines

Pre-school literacy and numeracy
One point of contention is the extent to which children in playgroups should be taught to read and write and develop numeracy. Teaching these skills may be a job for those who are trained, but consolidating them is a job for parents and other caring adults who have influence in a child's life. This may be achieved in a number of ways: reading to children, talking about letters, words and sounds, recognising numbers and numerical relationships. The crucial thing is that learning should be fun and a shared pleasure. Drawing, painting and play can all contribute to literacy and numeracy.

Home life helps too
Playgroups or nursery schools can provide invaluable help in the process, but often the best preparation for school is a positive attitude at home, with loving discipline, a stimulating environment and help in adjusting to the new demands and circumstances. Don't leave it all to the professionals!

How to help your child
☐ Choose a suitable playgroup — check out alternatives
☐ Select the best means of preparing for school
☐ Make starting school a regular topic of discussion at home
☐ Reinforce playgroup activities at home
☐ Be aware of any special needs that might emerge
☐ Concentrate on enjoyment rather than formal learning
☐ Try not to 'force' your child ahead

Punishments

Key points

- Teachers *in loco parentis*
- Reasonable punishment
- Types of sanction

In school teachers have some of the powers and responsibilities of parents — they are said to be *in loco parentis* — acting in the place of parents. This gives teachers the authority to administer *reasonable* punishments. The courts have decided what is reasonable; in general they have supported actions by teachers which are generally accepted, justified by the 'offence' and not excessive.

Since August 1987 corporal punishment in schools has been illegal — this means that any form of physical violence — caning, slippering, the use of the tawse and casual slapping may not be used under any circumstances. The most commonly used sanctions are:

- detention
- exclusion
- suspension
- expulsion
- other disciplinary procedures

Detention
Teachers may not detain pupils after the official end of the school day unless:
- their behaviour merits the punishment
- parents know in advance that the school operates a detention system
- proper notice (normally 24 hours) is given
- the detention is for a reasonable length of time
- adequate arrangements are made for the safe journey home of the child

Parents may refuse to allow their child to attend a detention; in this case the school will arrange an alternative punishment.

Exclusion
Technically children can only be excluded from school on medical grounds (see page 26). In reality children are instructed to stay away from school without the legal process of suspension. Exclusion may be used as a 'cooling off period' to help resolve a dispute.

On the other hand, since a head teacher has the power to make rules for the school then pupils and/or parents who refuse to accept them are excluding themselves. The way needs to be open for negotiation. Failure to reach agreement could result in a prosecution for non-attendance.

Suspension

This is a formal legal process by which a pupil is barred from school. The decision is the head teacher's, acting in consultation with the Governors and LEA.

Suspension may be used as a punishment in itself or as a prelude to further punishment. In the first instance it may be for three days — longer suspensions are possible but this does not remove the legal obligations on parents and LEA to educate the child.

Parents should be notified immediately if their child is suspended — the child's return to school is a matter for negotiation between school, LEA and parents.

Expulsion

When relationships between school and pupil break down completely then expulsion is sometimes seen as the final sanction. In fact a better approach would be to think of transfer to another school as the LEA still has the legal obligation to provide an education.

Other procedures

There are numerous disciplinary procedures used by schools, for example:

- **report cards** — the attendance, behaviour and work of a pupil is recorded at each lesson, checked by a senior teacher and often sent home for comment
- **removal of privileges** — loss of breaktime, and so on.
- **letters to parents** — giving information and asking for support
- **lines** — often used, but of doubtful value

Schools need to operate sanctions in the same way as any other social group. For sanctions to work:

- parents must be involved and supportive
- the punishment must be reasonable and appropriate
- in serious cases full consultation and negotiation must take place

How to help your child

- ☐ Support the school as much as you can
- ☐ Ask for detailed information if you are not satisfied
- ☐ Ensure that administrative procedures are followed
- ☐ Discuss disciplinary problems with your child
- ☐ Seek a meeting with the appropriate teacher if necessary

Records and References

Key points
- The nature of data stored
- Access and use
- Safeguarding interests
- Validity of references

Records
In the course of your child's education a vast amount of information will be collected and stored. Your child's 'file' will be opened when he/she starts school and continued until he/she leaves the school system. There are no set requirements as to what should or should not be kept. As a minimum the following topics will usually be covered:

Your Child's School Record

1   **Family and biographical** data — details of family, parents, contact in case of emergency etc

2   **Medical records** — basic medical information such as the School Health Service record card

3   **Academic progress** — results of attainment tests and copies of reports

4   **Accident** reports

5   **Copies of your letters** explaining absence and letters from the school to you

6   Accounts of **disciplinary** problems and incidents

Access to records
None of this is particularly controversial and you will probably have seen most of it at one time or another in different ways. However, you do not have an automatic right to see the complete records on demand and there is no process for challenging the accuracy of information.

Teachers may record opinions about you or your child which are subjective, based on limited knowledge and yet these views may be used in discussions with social services or educational psychologists.

It is up to the head teacher whether or not you can see your child's file. It is also up the head teacher to allow you to challenge any comments in the file. A refusal may not be sinister; schools may not have the time or clerical assistance to allow open access.

Protecting your child's interests

There is a growing body of opinion that files should be open and available (although this might simply create hidden files) but you can take certain steps:

● establish what the school policy is and, if access to files is denied, find out why

● keep your own copy of important letters to the school

● ensure that the school has up-to-date information about your domestic circumstances

If information is recorded on computer then it is available under the terms of the *Data Protection Act (1984).*

References

The same principle of secrecy often applies to references written by schools. These are often crucial to a student's chances of employment or admission to further and higher education.

It is worth remembering that only confidential references are regarded with any credibility.

There is no doubt that writing references for pupils is taken seriously by teachers and that they work to very high professional standards. However, mistakes of fact and interpretations can be made. If it becomes obvious that this has happened (for example, through comments made at a job interview), then the school should be contacted and a meeting arranged to clarify the information.

It must be said that references are usually requested and written under a guarantee of confidentiality and there is no right of access to them.

A good reference on leaving school needs to be earned as much as good examination results, and you can help your child to appreciate the importance of this.

How to help your child

☐ Check on your right of access to your child's file
☐ Ask to confirm the accuracy of the file
☐ Keep the school informed of changes in your circumstances
☐ Stress the importance to your child of a good reference

Records of Achievement

Key points

- Recognising all levels of achievement
- Graded tests
- Pupil involvement
- Potential value

Sometimes known as **pupil profiles,** records of achievement are an attempt to recognise the fact that many children leave school with no evidence of what they have achieved, and those who do obtain exam certificates have many other skills and qualities not covered by certificates.

If education is about more than examination results then there should be some means of expressing what has been experienced, learned and understood.

How to understand pupil profiles

A number of LEAs and schools have been developing profiling schemes and it is now DES policy that all secondary schools should produce records of achievement by 1990. The main purpose of records of achievement have been stated as:

- to provide **recognition** of what children have actually achieved in social and personal as well as academic terms

- to **motivate** towards achievable goals which have value in their eyes as well as to their parents and employers

- to **chart personal development** by recording information

- to act as a **document of record** incorporating all relevant information about a pupil's progress

Graded tests

At the same time as the introduction of profiling, LEAs are introducing graded tests, in maths, sciences and modern languages. These tests are taken when children reach the required level and are thus a record of what has actually been achieved. These tests are increasingly used for children who are unlikely to take GCSE exams.

Pupil involvement in profiling

One important development is the involvement of pupils in developing and writing their own profiles. This serves two purposes: it encourages pupils to become involved in assessing their own progress and so take greater responsibility for it. Secondly, it prevents over-subjective comments and fosters a sharing of views between pupils and staff.

A profile might include:

● details of public examination and graded test results

● levels of achievement in non-examined subjects, eg keyboard skills, practical abilities in CDT and home economics

● involvement in sporting activities, membership of teams and particular interests

● involvement in clubs and societies, hobbies and general interests

● participation in extra-curricular activities, visits, charity work and fund-raising events

● a personal appraisal of strengths and weaknesses, hopes and problems

Children are often disturbingly open about themselves and, if encouraged, can be ruthlessly honest and full of insight.

Value of profiles
Such profiles have enormous potential for children of all abilities. Potential employers as well as further and higher education bodies are almost always as interested in the person as in the qualifications. Indeed in many cases evidence of enthusiasm, social skills and a range of interests may be more revealing than a set of GCSE results.

If profiles are open then there should be no problems of accuracy. However, if a school is running, or plans to introduce, profiling then you should find out:

● who controls the system
● who has access to the profiles
● how and when the profiles are completed
● what use is to be made of them

There is no doubt that profiling imposes a considerable extra workload on teachers, but on the other hand the benefits of profiling are directly linked to the seriousness with which the profiles are taken by pupils, parents and employers.

How to help your child

☐ Obtain details of the school's policy on profiling
☐ Find out how the system works
☐ Make sure your son or daughter appreciates the importance of the system
☐ Take such profiles seriously when dealing with school-leavers in your own place of work

Religion and Education

Key points

- Understanding rather than instruction
- The right to opt out
- Acts of worship
- Church schools

There are three aspects to religion in the education sytem:

- religion in the curriculum
- worship
- church schools

Religion in the curriculum

Religion is the only compulsory element in the curriculum. The *1944 Education Act* requires the teaching of religion — but it does not compel children to receive it nor teachers to teach it. The Act allows parents to withdraw their children from religious education lessons (although children may not withdraw themselves) and teachers to refuse to teach them.

Local Education Authorities have produced 'agreed syllabuses' which these days will tend to concentrate on understanding religions rather than instruction in one particular doctrine. The emphasis will be on understanding world religions and examining moral and social issues.

In the modern curriculum RE lessons will often be combined with social studies or personal education.

Religion may also appear on the curriculum as an examination subject. It has the same value as any of the humanities subjects — history or social study — and is a genuine academic option.

Religious Education lessons

Modern RE lessons will often include the following topics:

Christianity — A knowledge of the main stories of the Bible, the principles of Christianity and a study of the history and practices of the Christian Churches.

Comparative Religion — A study of the world's other great religions; Islam, Buddhism, Hinduism and Judaism and how they differ from and are similar to Christianity.

Moral Issues — An exploration of the religious responses to war, crime, wealth and poverty and issues of public and personal morality.

Other Topics — Alternatives to religious faith, the work of charities, understanding the social and cultural aspects of religion.

Withdrawing your child from RE

To withdraw your child from compulsory RE lessons you should write to the head teacher stating your request. You should also find out what provision will be made for your child. Often they will have to sit at the back of the RE lesson and get on with their own work. If you wish them to spend the time studying your own religion then you should discuss this with the school.

Worship

The 1944 Act also requires a daily act of worship for the whole school. Parents have the right to withdraw their child if they wish. However, *assembly* has changed considerably — it may not be a daily event and will often be presented by the children themselves. It will often have a moral rather than explicitly religious message. Assemblies are also an important part of the corporate life of the school and exclusion from them may deprive your son or daughter of an important sense of belonging.

Church schools

Church Schools (also known as voluntary schools) are run by the religious denominations, most commonly the Church of England and Roman Catholic Church. There will usually be close links with the local church and the staff may be committed members of that church. The crucial difference between church and state schools is the emphasis upon the importance of religion in the life of the school and the fact that RE may be denominational.

The rights of parents to withdraw their children from assembly and RE lessons are the same in church schools as in state schools.

How to help your child

☐ Discuss the school's attitude to religion with your child
☐ Let the school know of your decision if you wish to opt out

Reports and Parents' Evenings

Key points

- Types and purpose of reports
- The information presented
- Reports and parents' evenings
- Follow-up with specific actions

Almost every school in the country provides some means of informing parents about the progress of their son or daughter. In most cases this involves the sending home of a written **school report** with the opportunity to discuss it at some form of open meeting.

By and large primary schools tend not to issue written reports but provide opportunities for parents to see their child's work and discuss it with the teacher. Where **diagnostic tests** are used for reading, mathematical ability and intellectual development, the head may invite parents in to discuss the results.

How to read school reports

Secondary schools have created a reporting system that is often complicated. There are no national guidelines as to what should be reported, how often or in what form. Reports may be:

- termly or annual
- in a booklet covering the whole school curriculum, all subjects on a single sheet or individual subject sheets
- with or without comments

The main functions of a report are to provide a record of progress, and to inform parents. To achieve this they will normally include the following information:

School Report

The subject being studied;

The band, set or stream your child is in;

An indication of the standard achieved in classwork, homework and tests or exams;

An indication of progress being made;

An indication of conduct

There may also be information about attendance, membership of clubs and societies, voluntary activities and so on.

All this information may be expressed as grades (usually A-E) or percentages, or there may just be a comment. Usually there will be a combination of these elements. Whatever system is used it should be explained on the report form; if not, then you should ask for clarification.

In general, reports are confidential between school and parent, and should not be used for other purposes without consultation.

Take advantage of parents' evenings

Reports by themselves are of little value — comments are usually brief and need development. If they are to be of value then they must lead to action. The best way to achieve this is through the parents' evening. You will need to make the best use of the limited time available and concentrate on these issues:

- **Clarification** of the report, eg
  'What does grade C actually mean?'
  '*Improving* compared to what?'
  'What does *hard work but little progress* imply for the future?'

- **Establishing the level** of work being done and the specific nature of any difficulties your child might be having.

- What are the **factors** contributing to your child's success or failure?

- **What needs to be done**, in practical terms, to remedy difficulties and reinforce success?

- **General factors** like homework, long-term potential and special support might also be discussed.

As well as consulting subject teachers, parents' evenings will also provide an opportunity to talk with pastoral staff — to obtain an overview — and, when appropriate, careers staff to obtain specialist advice.

It is important to remember that a good parents' evening is a two-way process and teachers will use them as an opportunity to express their own hopes and worries about your son or daughter.

To be of practical value parents' evenings should:

- result in practical outcomes
- be discussed in detail with your son or daughter

These principles apply equally to primary and secondary age children, but do bear in mind that, whilst each child is unique, to the teacher each child is one among at least 30.

Extract from a typical school report

NAME... Mark Bould .... D.O.B. 10/12/70......
TUTOR.... M' Blake ....
DATE...... July 1986 ....

SUBJECT	EFFORT	SET	ATTAINMENT	ATTENDANCE
				Good
ENGLISH LANGUAGE	1	O	A	PUNCTUALITY
				Good
ENGLISH LITERATURE	1	O	A	EFFORT grades reflect how hard we think
MATHEMATICS	1	1	A	your son/daughter is working in the
'CORE' SCIENCE				subject indicated i.e.
BIOLOGY	2	O/c	B	1. GOOD
WORLD STUDIES	1	O/c	A	2. Generally satisfactory
CREATIVE STUDIES				3. Poor.
PHYSICAL EDUCATION	1			SET (where used) indicates the
RELIGIOUS EDUCATION	2		A/D	general level for the teaching group i.e.
CAREERS				'O' Level
SOCIAL EDUCATION	1			C CSE
LANGUAGE	1	O/c	A	G City & Guilds
CITY & GUILDS				O/C Mixed.
HOME ECONOMICS				C/G Mixed.
COMMUNITY CARE				C/S Mixed
COMMERCIAL STUDIES				G/S Mixed.
ENGINEERING IND.				ATTAINMENT in a subject at the level
SOC & ENVIR.				indicated for the set is rated:-
ACTIVITIES				A. Good
				B. Generally Satisfactory.
				C. Poor.

	EFFORT	SET	ATTAINMENT	FORM TUTOR
OPTION 1	1	O/c	A	A good performance but the
OPTION 2	1	O/c	A	Biology mark does suggest
OPTION 3.	1		A	that Mark is working below his
HEAD OF YEAR/SENIOR TUTOR				potential in the subject.
Quite Pleasing		JClark		A good project report.

*On the basis of this report, what questions would you need to
ask, for example at a parents' evening (see p.99)?*

How to help your child

☐ Make sure you understand the report
☐ Use it as the basis for discussion at the parents' evening
☐ Follow up matters of concern with the school
☐ Discuss the report with your son or daughter

Parents' Evenings

These days parents' evenings are usually organised on an appointments system. Time is therefore limited and to make the best use of it you need to prepare issues for discussion.

1 Ask for information, in a way that you understand, about your child's
(a) **Position** — How are they working compared with the norm for their class, age, or exam group?

(b) **Performance** — Is the quality of work appropriate?

(c) **Potential** — What is your son's or daughter's longer term capability?

2 Find out about your child's behaviour and attitudes in the classroom and how these influence their work.

3 What is the teacher's perception of your son or daughter; does it differ from your own, and if so, how and why?

4 Is there any information that you need to pass on to the school?

5 What positive steps need to be taken by you, your child, and the teacher to remedy problems and build on success?

6 Remember that teachers respond to recognition and thanks.

School Meals

Key points

- Entitlement to free school meals
- Availability of school meals
- Developing healthy eating habits

If your income is such that you are entitled to **Family Income Supplement** then your child is entitled to free school meals. You will need to apply for this direct to the LEA, or through the school or the Education Welfare Officer.

LEAs are not legally obliged to provide meals and a number no longer do so. Most of the others have started schemes to make meals more attractive to pupils, and thus make the school meals service potentially self-financing. This trend has led to the introduction of cafeteria-style catering in many secondary schools and a wider choice in primary schools.

Healthy eating

This trend has coincided with a greater awareness of the importance of a **balanced diet** for children and young adults, emphasising the need for low-fat/high-fibre diets.

These two trends often appear to be pulling in opposite directions: cafeteria-style eating usually means convenience foods — fried and almost always with chips. What the customer wants is usually fat and sugar in various forms.

Apart from offering healthy alternatives there is little a school can do to change eating habits. School meals are not in fact a responsibility of the school. Science, home economics, PE and personal development lessons may stress the importance of healthy eating, but eating patterns at home will inevitably dominate.

An increasing number of school canteens are using wholemeal flour, offering fruit and salads and reducing the amount of fat-based and processed meat foods. However, this is balanced by the need of the school meals service to survive and this means pleasing the customer.

If you wish your child to have school meals, but using a **special diet**, then consult the head teacher or year head in the first instance.

Packed meals

Many children take packed meals to school. This is clearly an area where parental influence can be effective in creating a balanced diet. If children do take a packed meal then it should be more than just a snack. School burns up a great deal of energy and academic performance is often affected by inadequate nutrition (hence the importance of a good breakfast).

An ideal packed lunch would probably include the following items (according to taste!):

● sandwiches or rolls (made from wholemeal or high fibre bread) containing a protein filling
● fruit, nuts or raw vegetables
● sugar-based produce for energy
● suitable drink

Schools vary in their policies about drinks. It is worth finding out what sorts of containers are permitted.

It is worth remembering, too, that eating at lunchtime often gets in the way of playing or club activities and so the food needs to be attractive if it is not to be overlooked altogether. Children are also desperately concerned to conform with their peers — a sudden radical change in the content of the lunch-box might well be counter-productive.

How you can help
All parents are conscious of a link between their children's attitudes and behaviour and what they eat. Effective work at school depends upon regular, sensible eating habits almost as much as anything else so it is worth taking the trouble to foster good habits.

Examples of typical school meals

Menu A	Menu B
Cod in Batter	Chicken Curry
Chips	Wholegrain Rice
Swede	Peas
Green Beans	Oat Crunch Fruit Crumble
Jam Doughnut	Custard

Menu A does not fit in with guidelines for healthy eating being high in fat and low in fibre whereas Menu B is much better and healthier with less fat and more fibre.

How to help your child
☐ Check on your entitlement to free meals
☐ Encourage healthy eating habits at home
☐ Tell the school about special dietary needs
☐ Remember that school work is helped by a healthy and varied diet

School Rules and Uniforms

Key points

- Head teachers can make necessary rules
- Attendance assumes acceptance of rules
- Published rules are only a part of school discipline
- Observation of rules is part of the educational process

Head teachers are **legally responsible** for good order and discipline in their schools. Therefore any rules which the head feels are necessary will be supported by the courts if they are judged reasonable and necessary.

Bound by the rules

The law assumes that when you accept a place in a school for your child you automatically accept its rules — whether or not you have seen them. Some schools may ask you to sign a copy of the rules indicating that you accept them. This does not take away your **right to challenge** them if they are unreasonable but does mean that you cannot object to decisions enforced at a later stage.

Different schools, different rules

School rules are one of the ways in which schools develop their particular style and ethos. There is no one right approach and you need to consider the rules when choosing a school for your child.

Some schools will produce highly detailed rules — others broad principles stressing the need for cooperation and respect.

Rules will normally deal with the following matters:

- **Attendance** Times of arrival and departure, what constitutes lateness, procedures for leaving school during the day.

- **Use of premises** Areas of the school which are out of bounds or where pupils must be supervised (eg laboratories and workshops), use of the school during break times.

- **Dress** Description of the school uniform if there is one, or what constitutes acceptable and unacceptable dress — this may extend to shoes, jewellery and length of hair.

- **Behaviour** Movement around the school, tampering with equipment, banning certain items, eg knives, cigarettes, radios.

Such lists are not exclusive: just because a certain action is not listed does not mean that it is permissible! Rules cannot cover every eventuality and it is up to the head (or a teacher acting on his or her behalf) to decide what is unacceptable behaviour.

Thus the rules may not define or even mention **bullying** or **abusive behaviour** towards staff, but the head will be able to punish as he/she feels appropriate. The courts have supported heads and teachers in this respect almost without exception.

Teachers' powers

A teacher may confiscate items brought into school contrary to school rules or if they constitute a hazard. Such items must be returned to the pupil or, if appropriate, to his or her parents. In some cases, eg an offensive weapon, the police may be involved.

Teachers act with the authority of the head teacher and the law makes no distinction as long as the action is reasonable. If a school has a **prefect system** then the reasonable actions of prefects are binding upon pupils.

Understanding the rules

One of the best ways in which parents can help their child prepare for a new school is to go through the school rules and help their son or daughter understand them. It follows that school rules should be clear, simple and easy to understand. If you are uncertain then ask the school for clarification.

Grey areas

A possible area of confusion is the apparent variations in the expectations of teachers. Some will demand absolute silence and operate a highly regimented regime; others will be much more relaxed. Neither is right or wrong but simply a reflection of the teacher's own style and personality. Learning to cope with differing expectations is part of the educational process.

Be aware

The important thing is that schools and individual teachers should be consistent, fair and reasonable. If they are not, and you feel your child is being unfairly treated or victimised, then you should follow the **appeals** or **complaints** procedures outlined elsewhere.

How to help your child

- [ ] Obtain a copy of the rules
- [ ] Discuss them with your child
- [ ] Ask for clarification of any that are unclear
- [ ] Help your child observe them by maintaining a good home environment

Social Security

Key points

- Not the responsibility of the school
- Payments linked to school age
- Sources of advice

The fact that you have a child in full-time education means that you are entitled to certain benefits. These are the responsibility of the DHSS and not the education system. The Social Services department of your local council is probably the best place to get advice, although the Citizens' Advice Bureaux are a major source of information and there may well be local advice centres.

What follows is only a general guide. You will need to obtain expert guidance to find out what you are entitled to.

Child benefit

Child benefit is payable automatically from birth up to the age of 19 or until your child leaves full-time education, ie:

- is working full time and earning a wage
- receives supplementary benefit in their own right
- is on a YTS course
- receives a grant for further or higher education
- gets married

You must stop claiming the benefit in the week that your child's status changes.

Health benefits

Children of school age do not pay prescription charges, dental charges or have to pay for glasses. The appropriate practitioner will advise you on the procedure to follow.

Extra financial help

There are a number of benefits available to families with school age children which are based upon income and the number of children of school age in the family, eg:

- One Parent Benefit
- Family Income Supplement
- Guardian's Allowance
- Child's Special Allowances
- Supplementary Allowances

Details of your entitlement should be obtained from your local DHSS office. Leaflets are also available from post offices and by post from:

DHSS Leaflets Unit
PO Box 21
Stanmore
Middlesex
HA7 1AY

If you are receiving any form of supplementary benefit then you will normally be entitled to **free school meals**. However, you apply for these through the school or local education office, *not* the social services or the DHSS.

Your responsibility

Whatever form of benefit you apply for it is very important that you keep careful **records** of all the claims you make, and keep any letters you receive. These will help in sorting out disputes.

How much you tell the school of your situation is up to you — you may find individual teachers very helpful in making contacts for you and helping with the form-filling but this is up to them, it is not a required part of their job. Teachers will often work like your GP, referring you to a specialist for expert advice when they are no longer able to help.

For a full and excellent guide to the subject, refer to *How to Claim State Benefits* by Martin Rathfelder, published in this Series.

How to help your child

☐ Obtain expert advice
☐ Keep careful records and copies of all letters and documents
☐ Inform the school of changed circumstances if necessary

Special Educational Needs

Key points

- Children have a variety of needs
- Some have special educational needs
- The statementing process
- Special provision for children with learning difficulties

Nothing is more distressing than for parents to discover that their son or daughter is not 'normal'. Yet up to one in five of children in school may have some difficulty in fitting into school life. A variety of emotive words have been used to describe such children — slow, backward, remedial, handicapped, disturbed or disruptive, all of which are inaccurate. Children have varying abilities physically, emotionally and intellectually — the problem is recognising that there are varying levels of achievement and not one absolute standard. *Every* child is a unique individual with individual needs.

Special educational needs

The most important development in the education of such children was the *1981 Education Act* which introduced the idea of the **special educational needs** of children with learning difficulties. The Act removes any specific definition of handicap and replaces it with the notion of difficulties which are greater than for most children of the same age.

Statement of special educational needs

This raises the problem of how to define a child as having special educational needs. There will be a variety of possible causes including difficulties in vision, hearing, speech, physical and mental handicap.

The central part of the new provision is the process of generating a **statement**.

The LEA

The statement process may be started by the LEA or parents. If parents request a statement then the LEA may not unreasonably refuse it — and parents have the right of appeal to the Secretary of State if the LEA does refuse.

The LEA may carry out an **assessment** on a child over 2, even if the parents object. However, the LEA must take parents' views into account and accept evidence offered on their behalf. Parents have a right to see all written evidence; they also have an obligation to ensure that their child attends any examination which is considered necessary.

The school

The statement from the school consists of four parts:

1. A description of the child in terms of his or her physical state, emotional and social well being, ability to learn and communicate, interest and behaviour.

2. A list of the special educational facilities and resources necessary to help in the development of physical control and coordination, intellectual skills such as language development, and social skills.

3. A description of the type of education which is most appropriate in the light of points 1 and 2.

4. An outline of any extra facilities which may be necessary.

The completed statement

When the statement is completed parents have a right to comment on it before it is finalised. This can all be stressful as it involves a lengthy and complex process on top of the difficulties which started the process in the first place. Finally there is no guarantee that the LEA will be able to meet all the needs identified in the statement. The 1981 Act increased the responsibilities of LEAs but did not create extra resources to meet them.

Integration

One possible result of completing the statement process is the integration of children with special needs into 'normal' schools.

Handicapped children can benefit enormously from contact with other children who in turn can also benefit. However, this involves careful preparation by the school, the provision of special resources and possibly extra staffing. Experience seems to suggest that integration works well with younger children but is less successful as they get older.

Integration can only work if there are strong and real links between home and school and full use is made of specialist services. Special needs may be social as well as medical in origin — the ability of schools to cope is directly linked to the resources available. If those resources are not available then special schools may be the best answer.

How to help your child

☐ Recognise that there is no stigma in having special needs
☐ Accept specialist advice but ask for explanation
☐ Make sure that the statementing process is fully explained to you
☐ Work with the school and your child to help achieve full integration
☐ Discuss the process with your child

Sport in Schools

Key points

- Social and educational purposes
- Competitive or non-competitive
- Compulsory or optional
- Parental involvement

Most people involved in schools would accept that education includes physical as well as social and intellectual development. Yet few subjects in the curriculum generate as much enthusiasm, or as much active hostility, as PE and games.

Physical education in one form or another is one of the few subjects to be found across the age range and in almost every type of school.

The philosophy of physical education

In terms of educational development sport in schools can lead to the development of a wide range of skills and activities not directly linked to the games themselves. Physical coordination, confidence, self-esteem as well as cooperation and learning to work in groups are all possible outcomes.

A broader view would see physical education as a part of health education, laying foundations for healthier living in adult life.

A further aspect is what is sometimes described as **education for leisure**, recognising that the proper use of leisure time is as important, in a different way, as **education for employment**.

In **primary schools** the opportunities for such developments are limited by the expertise of staff and the availability of resources. However, the use of activity equipment, imaginative approaches to games and play and the use of resources outside the school can all enhance children's enjoyment.

A range of opportunities

In the **secondary school** there are far greater opportunities for a diversity of activities. Indeed the whole approach has changed in many schools, shifting the emphasis away from all children doing the same activity to a range of options. 'Games' thus becomes a matter of choice based on interest. Football is available alongside archery, netball with orienteering. However, this approach totally depends upon the availability of resources, expertise of teachers and often extra funding.

Schools are not financed to offer a full range of sporting activities and in some cases activities may involve an extra charge. One positive way in which parents can help is to offer their time and expertise to supplement that of teaching staff. However, this depends on LEA and school policy, holding recognised qualifications and being absolutely clear about insurance cover.

Competitive sport

Two issues are inevitably raised when discussing the place of physical education in schools: the place of competitive sport, and whether sport should be compulsory.

Competitive sport has been questioned by some teachers and administrators as developing unhealthy attitudes and reinforcing some of the worst aspects of professional sport. This is very much a matter of school policy in response to LEA guidelines. However, it ought to be a matter for debate and could be discussed through the PTA or with parent-governors.

Compulsory sport

For children who are not competent at any sport, and for many in the fourth and fifth year of secondary schooling, compulsory games are often unacceptable. The relevance of games is questioned, given all the pressures of examination courses and the demands of adolescence.

Play your part

Parental support is crucial to sporting activities through positive attitudes, the provision of appropriate kit, support and interest. Problems with PE and games deserve as much attention as any other part of the curriculum.

How to help your child

☐ Find out the philosophy of the school
☐ Find out in detail what options are available
☐ Offer your help to the school (if qualified)
☐ Build on your child's interests
☐ Take an interest in your child's involvement in school sporting activities and show encouragement

Trips and Visits

Key points

- Educational importance of trips and visits
- Good organisation by the school
- Rules and regulations

School trips and visits are an important part of the educational process. They may arise directly out of the curriculum — visits to museums, art galleries, sports events, theatres, field trips — or they may be more broadly educational — foreign holidays and adventure holidays, for example.

Taking a party of children away for the day to a local museum or for ten days to North Africa imposes considerable demands upon the teachers involved, since they are totally responsible for the well-being and safety of your child.

Most LEAs have **codes of good practice** for the organisers of school trips and may not allow a visit to proceed unless it meets various requirements. Even so parents should satisfy themselves on certain points.

Consent

Any form of excursion from school should be on the basis of your approval, usually given by signing a form which indicates the nature of the visit, any special activities, duration, cost and names of the organising teachers, travel agents and/or tour company.

Indemnity letters

Indemnity letters which seek to protect journey organisers from claims arising from accidents or negligence do not prevent parents issuing a writ if it is felt that the organisers have been negligent.

Insurance

Most LEAs insist upon appropriate insurance for all visits and you should find out from the organisers exactly what cover has been arranged.

Medical problems

You should inform the organisers well in advance of any particular medical problems your child has. They would be justified in refusing to take your child if they felt that unacceptable risks might arise. As teachers are *in loco parentis* on the trip then they may take such decisions about medical treatment as are necessary. You may be asked to sign a **general consent form**. If you are a Jehovah's Witness or Christian Scientist then you must discuss possible medical problems with the organising staff.

Payment

Trips and visits are becoming very expensive. You should establish at the outset the full cost of the visit (including spending money). Ensure that you get a signed receipt for each payment made. Follow the organisers' guidelines on how much spending money to give your child.

Discipline

Organisers are perfectly within their rights in refusing to take children whose behaviour they do not trust. Preliminary information about the visit should indicate policy on dress, smoking, drinking etc. In the final analysis children may be sent home.

Safety

Expeditions and sporting tours raise special issues of safety. Any form of 'outward bound' or 'wild country' activity should only be led by qualified outdoor education staff. You should satisfy yourself that all aspects are covered.

Organisation

A well organised school visit will ensure that:

● you have full information about the visit, where your child is and when
● the organisers have your details if they need to contact you urgently
● arrangements for collection of children are clear and understood
● you have a contact name and telephone number

Customs

Children under 17 are not allowed to bring alcohol or tobacco products into this country — some souvenirs may attract customs duty and VAT.

Teachers are usually very skilled and experienced in organising and leading school visits. Schools often use specialist travel companies who have considerable expertise in organising school parties. As a parent you need to satisfy yourself that the points above have been covered and to ensure that your own son or daughter understands their responsibilities.

How to help your child

☐ Allow your child to go on trips whenever possible
☐ Ensure that you are happy with every aspect of organisation
☐ Satisfy yourself that your child understands all the arrangements
☐ Help make the trip a learning process in every way

School Trips and Visits

Before signing a form consenting to your child going on a school trip (and your approval should be sought for every trip) you should check that you have the following information.

1   The name of the staff member in charge.

2   The number of staff on the trip.

3   The ratio of staff to pupils (normally a maximum of 1:15).

4   The precise itinerary showing location, date and time.

5   Travel arrangements.

6   Insurance and medical provision.

7   The telephone number of a contact in school.

8   The method of payment and arrangements for receipts.

9   Rules for spending money.

10 Rules about smoking and drinking.

5
Helping Your Child's Development

The work that children do in schools is guided by teachers who have been trained in two important ways: firstly in the skills of actually **teaching and helping** children to learn, and secondly in the detailed **specialist knowledge** of the subjects they teach. When this is combined with experience and special resources, parents could be tempted to think they have little to offer in addition.

This is not the case, but parents are in a better position to help their children if they have some knowledge of the differences between intelligence and ability, and the ways in which children learn.

Intelligence and ability

There is a great deal of mythology about intelligence. There are a number of tests designed to measure the amount of intelligence a child possesses. These are known as IQ **(Intelligence Quotient)** tests and VRT **(Verbal Reasoning Tests)**. These tests are designed to indicate a child's *potential* to learn rather than their ability to remember, and they often reflect the ability to take the tests of verbal and logical skills rather than intelligence as such.

It might be more accurate to see intelligence as one of a range of human abilities which include physical, mechanical, artistic, personal and social skills. There should be no **ranking of abilities** but rather a recognition that thinking is not limited to academic subjects and can apply to any form of activity. Reading and understanding Shakespeare is qualitatively no different from learning to understand and apply a practical skill.

We need to see achievement not in terms of a ranking, then, but rather in each individual child reaching the maximum of which they are capable in the sphere for which they are best suited.

Developing ability

There are two important elements in ensuring that your child can reach his/her maximum potential:

- recognising ability
- helping to develop ability

Abilities will be shown in a variety of ways and it is only a sensitive understanding by parents and teachers that will allow them to flourish. Forcing children into a mould is guaranteed to repress natural interests and talents. Abilities will emerge through obsessions, interests and enthusiasms. Equally such phases will change and pass; this is a perfectly natural process, part of learning, exploring and development.

We all work best when we believe that our efforts are going to lead to an outcome of value. For a child that outcome may be interest, excitement, natural curiosity, a chance for recognition, admiration or simply pleasure. What is important is that you provide reinforcement by encouraging, praising and respecting. Progress for a child results from a feeling that what they are doing is important to them and to you. In practical terms this means showing interest by asking for information, making time to find out and most importantly respecting genuine effort.

That effort might appear to be directed towards a range of non-educational ends but an interest in cars can stimulate the desire to read, and an interest in animals can teach caring and responsibility. Education is a cumulative process in which nothing is wasted. Children need help in recognising that which is good and creative and that which is negative and destructive. But it is necessary to experience in order to understand and learn, and learning is often a shared process.

This does not mean 'telling' but rather helping to understand by questioning. *'Tell me why*?' can be the most important part of the learning process.

Where to Get Help

You will find the addresses of local schools in the telephone directory under the name of the education authority which will also give details of the education offices. Yellow Pages have an entry for Schools and Colleges, and for Local Government.

Your local library should be able to give you this information or will have a copy of the *Education Year Book* which has details of each school in the country. They will also have details of the local Citizens Advice Bureaux.

Organisations and Government Bodies

Advisory Centre for Education
18 Victoria Park Square
London E2 9BP
Tel: (01) 980-4596

Child Action Poverty Group
1 Macklin Street
London WC2B 5NH
Tel: (01) 242 3225

Children's Legal Centre
20 Compton Terrace
London N1 2UN
Tel: (01) 359 6251

Citizens' Advice Bureaux
110 Drury Lane
London
WC2B 5SW
Tel: (01) 836 9231

Commission for Racial Equality
Elliot House
10-12 Allington Street
London
SW1E 5EH
Tel: (01) 828 7022

Department of Education and Science
Elizabeth House
York Road
London SE1 7PH
Tel: (01) 934 9000

Equal Opportunities Commission
Overseas House
Quay Street
Manchester M3 3HN
Tel: (061) 833 9244

Gingerbread
(Association for One Parent Families)
35 Wellington Street
London WC2
Tel: (01) 240 0953

The Independent Schools Information Service (ISIS)
56 Buckingham Gate
London SW1E 6AH
Tel: (01) 630 8793

National Association of Governors
and Managers
81 Rustlings Road
Sheffield S11 7AB
Tel: (0742) 662467

National Confederation of Parent-
Teacher Associations
43 Stonebridge Road
Northfleet
Gravesend
Kent
Tel: (0474) 60618

GCE exam boards

Associated Examining Board (AEB)
Wellington House
Station Road
Aldershot
Hants GU11 1BQ
Tel: (0252) 25551

Cambridge University Local
Examinations Syndicate
Syndicate Buildings
17 Harvey Road
Cambridge CB1 2EU
Tel: (0223) 61111

Joint Matriculation Board (JMB)
Manchester M15 6EU
Tel: (061) 273 2565
(Syllabuses and Regulations from:
J Sherratt & Sons, Publishers,
Park Road, Timperley, Cheshire)

Northern Ireland Schools
Examinations Council
Beechill House
42 Beechill Road
Belfast BT8 4RS
Tel: (Belfast) 704666

Oxford & Cambridge Schools
Examination Board
Elsfield Way
Oxford OX2 8EP
Tel: (0865) 54421 *or*

Pre-School Playgroup Association
Alford House
Averling Street
London SE11 5DH
Tel: (01) 582 8871

Brook House
10 Trumpington Street
Cambridge CB2 1QB
Tel: (0223) 64326

Oxford Delegacy of Local
Examinations
Ewart Place
Summertown
Oxford OX2 7BZ
(Tel: (0865) 54291

Southern Universities Joint Board
for School Examinations
Cotham Road
Bristol
Avon BS6 6DD
Tel: (0272) 736042

University of London Schools
Examinations Council
66-72 Gower Street
London WC1E 6EE
Tel: (01) 636 8000
(Publications Department:
50 Gordon Square,
London WC1H OPJ)

Welsh Joint Education Committee
245 Western Avenue
Cardiff CF5 2YX
Tel: (0222) 561231

GCSE exam boards
The GCSE regional boards are made up of the following individual boards
and further information is available from any of them — the addresses
of the GCE boards have been given above.

London & East Anglia Examining Group
East Anglian Examination Board (CSE), London Regional Examining
Board (CSE), University of London Schools Examinations Council (GCE).

Midland Examining Group
Cambridge University Local Examinations Syndicate (GCE), East Midland
Regional Examinations Board (CSE), Oxford & Cambridge Schools
Examination Board (GCE), Southern Universities Joint Board for School
Examinations (GCE), West Midlands Examinations Board (CSE).

Northern Examining Association
Associated Lancashire Schools Examining Board (CSE), Joint Matricula-
tion Board (GCE), North Regional Examinations Board (CSE), North-
West Regional Examinations Board (CSE), Yorkshire & Humberside
Regional Examinations Board (CSE).

Northern Ireland Schools Examinations Council
(as GCE)

Southern Examining Group
Associated Examining Board (GCE), Oxford Delegacy of Local Examina-
tions (GCE), South-East Regional Examinations Board (CSE), Southern
Regional Examinations Board (CSE), South-Western Examinations Board
(CSE).

Welsh Joint Education Committee
(as GCE)

Other exam boards

City & Guilds of London Institute
76 Portland Place
London W1N 4AA
Tel: (01) 580 3050

Pitman Examinations Institute
Catteshall Manor
Godalming
Surrey GU7 1UU
Tel: (04868) 5311

Royal Society of Arts
    Examinations Board (RSA)
John Adam Street
Adelphi
London WC2N 6EZ
Tel: (01) 839 2366

Glossary

This glossary includes words and terms which are in regular use in schools and not defined elsewhere in this book.

Aide A person appointed to help a teacher in a nursery or recognised class who is usually qualified as a nursery nurse or welfare assistant. They may also be appointed where children with special needs are integrated into a normal school.

Bases Open-plan schools may have class bases or classrooms may have bases for groups of children.

Basic Skills Literacy and numeracy or the three Rs — reading, writing and arithmetic.

Child-Centred Methods Children are allowed to learn by following up their own interests rather than following the teachers' directions. This may also involve the discovery method of learning where children establish basic ideas for themselves.

Community School Where a school is seen as a part of the life of the whole community and its resources are used for a wide variety of activities, eg crèche facilities, pensioners' lunch clubs, youth clubs and evening classes.

Computer Literacy Familiarity with the operating procedures and potential uses of personal computers.

Environmental Studies/Humanities Terms used to describe an integrated approach to the teaching of history, geography, RE and aspects of maths, English and art. Widely used in the upper classes of primary schools and first years of the secondary school.

Flash Cards Pieces of cardboard with words or numbers printed on them to help children learn and identify them.

General Science An integrated approach to science teaching linking physics, biology and chemistry.

Home Teaching Qualified teachers visiting children at home to ensure their education continues in cases of suspension, lengthy illness, pregnancy.

Information Technology The use of computers and word processors to deal with a wide range of data.

Integrated Day Where there is no formal timetable and so the teacher is able to develop a topic to its logical conclusion.

Lower and Upper School Terms used to describe years 1-3 and 4-6 in secondary schools.

Modern Maths An approach to the teaching of mathematics which concentrates on children understanding the 'why' as well as the 'how' of mathematical processes.

Multicultural Education A systematic attempt to recognise in all parts of the curriculum that Britain is a society made up of a mixture of races, languages and religions.

Reception Class The first class your child will enter in nursery or primary school which concentrates as much on learning to be at school as on formal lessons.

Remedial Correctly applied, a term which indicates a need for extra help, whether across the full range of subjects or just in one area.

Rising Fives The policy of admitting children to school in the term before their fifth birthday.

Social Service Sometimes referred to as community service, the means by which a school involves pupils in the local community helping the elderly or any other group that might benefit.

Team Teaching Where several teachers work together to teach a large number of children, allowing greater opportunities for specialisation and individual help.

Educational Acronyms

BTEC	Business and Technician Education Council
CDT	Craft, Design, Technology
CFE	College of Further Education
CHE	College of Higher Education
CNAA	Council for National Academic Awards
CPVE	Certificate of Pre-Vocational Education
CSE	Certificate of Secondary Education
DES	Department of Education and Science
FE	Further Education
FHE	Further and Higher Education
GCE	General Certificate of Education
GCSE	General Certificate of Secondary Education
HE	Higher Education
HMI	Her Majesty's Inspectorate
ILEA	Inner London Education Authority
IQ	Intelligence Quotient
ISIS	Independent Schools Information Service
JTS	Job Training Scheme
LEA	Local Education Authority
MSC	Manpower Services Commission
PE	Physical Education
PTA	Parent-Teacher Association
RE	Religious Education
RSA	Royal Society of Arts
SEN	Special Educational Needs
TVEI	Technical and Vocational Educational Initiative
VRT	Verbal Reasoning Test
YTS	Youth Training Scheme

Further Reading

Periodicals

Education (Weekly)
Times Educational Supplement (weekly)
Times Higher Education Supplement (weekly)

General books

How To Pass Exams without Anxiety, David Acres (Northcote House 1987)
How to Choose a Private School, Tony Attwood (Northcote House 1988)
How to Claim State Benefits, Martin Rathfelder (Northcote House 1987)
How to Get That Job, Joan Fletcher (Northcote House 1987)
How to Survive at College, David Acres (Northcote House 1987)
Successful Exam Technique, David Cocker (Northcote House 1987)
How To Choose a School C. Itzin (Methuen 1985)
A Parent's Guide to Education B. Taylor (Hodder & Stoughton 1983)
Where to Look Things Up, A-Z of Sources, E. Wallis (ACE, 1983)
How Children Fail, John Holt (Penguin 1980)

Reference books

British Qualifications (Kogan Page, annual)
Gabbitas-Thring Guide to Independent Further Education (Northcote House, annual)
Education Authorities Directory and Annual (School Government Publishing Company)
Education Year Book (Longman, annual)
Directory of Further Education (CRAC, annual)

Index

religion in schools, 50
religious education, 96
revision, 54-55
rising fives, 88
Royal Society of Arts, 53, 119

safety, responsibility for, 20, 21
School Health Service, 74
school meals, 50, 66, 102-3, 107
school prospectus, 17, 34, 38
schools, types of, 10
Scotland, schools in, 13
secondary schools, organisation of, 15
sex discrimination, 31, 50, 77
special needs statement, 22, 108-109
sport, 57, 110-111
subject choice, 76, 80
subjects,

primary, 44-45
secondary, 46-47
suspension, 22

teachers' powers, 105
tertiary colleges, 11, 81
travel to school, 20, 26, 66
truancy, 26

uniform, 50, 67, 104

voluntary schools, 10, 97

Wales, schools in, 13
worship, 97

Youth Training Scheme, 81

How To... Books
Opening Doors of Opportunity

A major series of self-help paperbacks packed with valuable information on new opportunities in today's fast-changing world. Each of these user-friendly handbooks gives clear up-to-date information and advice, prepared by experts, and complete with checklists for action and self-assessment material. The guides will save you time and money by supplying essential information which is often hard to find.

Helpfully clear layout with illustrations and cartoons, glossary, useful sources, index. Each 215 x 135mm, £4.95 approx.

You can't afford to miss the 'How To . . . series'

How to Get That Job Joan Fletcher
A guide for job hunters of all ages.
0 7463 0326 2

How to Pass Exams Without Anxiety David Acres
A step by step guide to removing stress and achieving success in exams at every level.
0 7463 0334 3

How to Live and Work in Australia Laura Veltman
The unique handbook for all those considering employment and residence 'Down Under'.
0 7463 0331 9

How to Live and Work in America Steve Mills
Packed with new ideas on home life, leisure, travel, social and business opportunities.
0 7463 0323 8

How to Choose a Private School Tony Attwood
Essential reading for all parents wishing to review the options available for their children in private education.
0 7463 0522 2

How to Claim State Benefits Martin Rathfelder
Making sense of the system.
0 7463 0505 2

How to Raise Business Finance Peter Ibbetson
A down-to-earth guide for the self-employed and small business needing financial assistance.
0 7463 0338 6

Dozens more titles in preparation. For details please contact Dept BPA.

Northcote House Publishers Ltd., Harper & Row House, Estover Road, Plymouth PL6 7PZ, United Kingdom.
Tel: Plymouth (0752) 705251 Telex: 45635.

ew General Certificate of Secondary Education (GCSE) replaces
ɔld GCE O-levels and CSE examinations in 1988. The new
scheme contains many important new features, including teaching and
study methods and assessment. This new paperback will be vital
reading for all parents who wish to understand the full implications
for their own children of secondary school age.

Allan Matten is Senior Assistant Secretary to the Associated
Examining Board and GCSE Coordinator for the new Southern
Examining Group.

£4.95 paperback, 96pp. 0 7463 0526 5

Successful Exam Technique
David Cocker

Attractively laid out in self-contained spreads, this remarkably easy-
to-use paperback breaks new ground for those thousands of students
who want to develop a really winning revision and examination
technique. With its quick reference headings, graphics, cartoons,
checklists and summaries, it will be the one absolutely essential
purchase for examination candidates throughout the English-speaking
world, who want down-to-earth help and want it fast.

David Cocker BSc PhD CChem MRSA, a young Post-Doctoral
Fellow and University Demonstrator, has himself successfully sat
some 100 main examination papers. This remarkable experience has
enabled him to develop and test a really comprehensive set of
techniques, with students, now brought together in **Successful Exam
Technique.**

£3.95 paperback, 96pp. Illustrated. 0 7463 0348 3

The Gabbitas-Thring Guide to Independent Further Education in the UK 1987-88
Edited by Len Shaw BEd MA MBIM

Completely authoritative and up-to-date, this important new edition
of the annual illustrated **Guide** provides parents, teachers, careers
advisers and students with a really comprehensive sourcebook on this
growing independent sector in British education today. With its 400
detailed entries, and informative articles by leading specialist
contributors, the **Guide** meets a real need for consumer information
on private schools, colleges and training establishments in every area
of study from GCE to secretarial, and technical to domestic arts.

£9.95 paperback, 150pp. Illustrated. 0 7463 0514 1

Northcote House Publishers Ltd, Harper & Row House, Estover Road,
Plymouth PL6 7PZ, United Kingdom. Tel: (0752) 705251. Telex:
45635. Fax: (0752) 777603.